Opa's Rhyme

Mark Fralick

Opa's Rhyme

Artwork by: Magdalena Solowianiuk

See us at: www.opasrhyme.com

ISBN: 0991574206
ISBN-13: 978-0-9915742-0-9

For my lads, Jack and Sam

Be the best version of *you*. The best version of you is *not* some version that others seek. Work only to be the best version of the person *you* wish to be. Life is full of compromises, but don't falter on this. Failure in this most paramount of things will, almost certainly, make for regret. Decide *who you are* or *the person you wish to be* and 'lean into it' - even, and especially, if it means leaning into headwinds.

And love!

CONTENTS

ACKNOWLEDGMENTS

I would like to acknowledge some of the people who helped me with this project or were part of the inspiration for it.

First, without my wife Patti, none of this would have been possible. She is the glue that holds our family together and the constant in my life. Patti inspires me every day and helped me craft this story.

Thank you to all that have helped with this project. I really do appreciate it. Additionally, I've been fortunate to have a few individuals inspire me with their strength and resilience. Special thanks to my mother Joyce Fralick, my grandfather Clayton Fralick, Vi Weber, Mr. Lawrence Stehling, Jim Hoefflin, Scott Stewart and my brother David for being sources of inspiration to me.

Finally, one cannot acknowledge enough the sacrifices made by the men and women of the US Armed Forces. In particular, I'd like to acknowledge the original group of Sea Bees of the US Navy. They were older, many in their forties with growing families of their own, when called to serve. Yet they served with bravery and distinction, building the ports and airfields allowing the US military to push to victory in the Pacific theater during WWII. They are, truly, an example of the *Greatest Generation.*

Mark Fralick

1

SNOWDRIFTS

Jake eyed the snowdrift in front of him. "Now *there's* a nice one," he mumbled. Cocooned in a blue snowsuit, mittens, and his beloved Green Bay Packers hat, he struggled forward, his legs lost in the snow. Silently, like a cat hunting its prey, Jake crouched; ready to pounce. With all his might, he lunged forward, hurling his entire body in the air. Face-first, his dive took him deep into the drift.

Blinking the snow out of his eyes, Jake shouted, "Oh, did you see that, Bill?" mocking an announcer's voice he had heard on TV. Blessed with a vivid and active imagination, Jake often made up commentaries about things and happenings around him.

"Yeah Bob, it was a beaut! There aren't many ten year-olds that are going to try a dive like that. Must be about an 11.8 degree of difficulty!" he continued, shaking the snow from his face. Laughing, he surveyed the damage he inflicted upon the snowdrift.

"Jake!" he heard from a distance. "Jake! Time to come in," it was his mom.

"Okay Mom!" he called. "Hmmm," he whispered. Surprised that she called him in so early, he started back to the house. "Oh well," he sighed, retracing his footsteps through the snow.

Jake loved being outside in the winter, though most of his friends didn't. The air just seemed so much cleaner, the sky brighter, and the stars somehow shinier.

Approaching the shoveled sidewalk of their home, Jake looked up at the house. He quickly scanned the windows of the modest two-story home, looking for any sign of his mother's gaze.

Jake's home, an older Cream City brick bungalow, showed few signs of its age. As in many parts of Milwaukee, this style of home dotted the neighborhood - *Cream City* referring to both their color and Milwaukee's bygone nickname.

Jake often wondered if someone just showed up one day, a long time ago, and said, 'I think I'll build 27 houses that all look the same right here.' Jake's family had lived in this house for more years than Jake could count. In fact, his mother grew up in this very house.

Not tall for a two-story home, old bungalows like Jake's used space well and did not have attics. The small windows and simple trim allowed them to withstand the harsh Midwest winters with ease.

Jake's house was, without doubt, the finest example of a Cream City bungalow on the block. But today the thing you most noticed was the icicles lined up like little soldiers.

Clinging below the many rooflines of Jake's home,

they glistened and sweated - even in the cold, cold air.

Deciding the *coast was clear*, Jake sized up the spot of level snow situated between him and the sidewalk. In one motion, he spun his body and thrust it to the ground. In a sudden burst of energy, he repeatedly shot his arms outward from his body and at the same time moving his legs into the shape of a *V*.

Jake lie motionless in the snow for a long moment. The sky above him seemed impossibly blue, and the clouds as cold and white as the snowdrift he just destroyed.

"There!" he said after a time, pulling himself from the snow and stomping his boots as he reached the sidewalk. He looked back at his creation. Smiling, he examined the form of his newest snow angel. 'Not bad,' he thought, opening the door to the house.

Mark Fralick

2

NEWS

"Slam!" went the door, as Jake stepped onto the welcome mat, just inside the front door of his house. Family pictures, just to the left of the door, bounced and nearly flew off their perch as the jolt and rush of air hit them.

"Jacob Samuel, what do we know about that door?" called his mom from behind him.

"Oops! We know we shouldn't slam it?" Jake responded in a half question, as he turned in the direction of his mother's voice.

"Thank you," she said, as she looked at him. "Looks like a successful outing," noting the snow caked into the fabric of his hat, clinging to his hair, and packed into every fold of his snowsuit. His chubby red cheeks glistened with half-melted snow.

Jake's mom, Julia, always seemed to look good. Her deep blue eyes and blond hair turned heads everywhere she went. Her moves, fluid and graceful, did not belie her years and years of training as a figure skater. Julia's face expressed every thought; she didn't hold back her feelings.

If there is one thing Jake knows about his mom, it's that she laughs loudly. She lived life in a big way; nothing was ever halfway.

Jake's mom loved that Jake liked the outdoors. 'So few kids,' she thought, 'want to go outside and just play.'

The lot her father built this home on had big beautiful trees, great hiding places, and a big open space between the house and the garage in the back.

She had great memories of the time spent in this yard with her dad and friends. She hoped the same for Jake.

"Yep, three really big ones – did you see?" he responded, his deep green eyes smiling.

"Yes, sweetheart, I saw that last one. A spectacular dive; must have been a big degree of difficulty on that one!" she said to him, beaming with genuine pride.

"Yep," Jake laughed, "that was a whopper!"

"Jake," she said, as she walked toward him, "we have something we need to talk about." She leaned down to help him out of his snow gear.

"You mean about that last snow angel I made, but it was on the way in," he whispered apologetically, thinking she had seen him.

"No, sweetheart, it's about your grandfather," she whispered back.

"Opa?" he asked, surprised.

"Yes, Jake, Opa is coming to stay with us for a little while. We're going to the airport tomorrow to pick him up. He's…"

"How long will he stay?" Jake interrupted.

Jake's mother was silent for a moment. "Just for a

little while…" she responded, as her eyes, usually as bright and blue as the sky on these cold winter days, dimmed with sadness. "Dinner in a few minutes, sweetheart," she said, as she stood and walked slowly to the kitchen.

Mark Fralick

3

THE MAN OF THE FAMILY

Tssss... Jake heard an odd sound coming from the kitchen a minute later as he unwrapped himself and hung his winter gear. Tall for his age, he had a solid, slightly heavy build. His thick, dark blond hair, now flat and wet from the melting snow and ice, glistened as he hung his hat on the hook near the front door.

Tssss... He heard the sound again. Quietly, Jake walked to the edge of the kitchen. While just large enough for the family's old dinette table flanked by four chairs, the kitchen was certainly the hub of activity in their house.

Jake's mother, facing away from him, tended the covered pans on the stove. As she turned to fetch a fork from the counter, he saw a tear running down her face. As if in slow motion, it cascaded down her cheek - leaving a faint trail on her skin.

Tssss, it cried, as it fell from her chin to the cover of a simmering pot, evaporating as quickly as the sound faded.

Peeking from behind the half-wall that separated the kitchen from the rest of the house, Jake whispered, "Mom? Mom, what's the matter?"

"Honey," she started, "just some grown-up things, nothing to worry about." Jake could tell she was trying to do her *happy* look.

"Okay," he said, "but you always say that I'm the *man* of the family. Maybe I can help."

She smiled, so proud of whom this young man was becoming. "You *are* the man of this family, Jake," she said.

She looked for a moment into Jake's thoughtful green eyes. Wise, somehow wise beyond his years, were these eyes. He squinted when deep in thought, just like his grandfather, but also when he laughed. He squinted now.

"But sometimes there are things that the grown-ups have to deal with, that children, even if they are the *m*an of the family, don't need to worry about. Tomorrow we'll go to the airport and pick up your grandfather. You'll need to share your room with Opa and sleep in your sister's room for a while."

"Oh," Jake said, sounding very disappointed. "Do I have to? Girls smell funny!"

"Jacob! First of all, girls do not smell funny!" Jake's mom laughed.

"A lot of them do," Jake whispered.

"And second of all," his mother continued, paying no attention to the comment, "Emily *is* only four years old and not much trouble. She would really love it if you stayed with her for a little while. Sometimes, being a young man means making sacrifices. Now…no matter what you say, I know you love your sister. So, it shouldn't really be *that* big of a sacrifice, should it?"

"Okay, okay!" Jake giggled. "But I'm going to let you know if she smells!"

Jake's mom couldn't help but laugh. "Now wash up, Mister!" she said, as she steered Jake's head toward the washroom. 'What a great boy,' she thought, smiling to herself.

She often worried about her boy - as moms do. She told herself that all she wanted was to raise this little guy to be a good and happy person. But she couldn't help worrying that Jake hasn't had enough time to just be a kid.

It had been a year since Jake's father's been gone. 'Too young to lose your father,' she thought sadly. Jake's sister, Emily, hadn't even gotten to know him.

That, alone, was sad. But it was even worse for Jake. Boys need their fathers. Jake, never having problems before, was not doing well in school. He just didn't seem like the boy he once was.

"Maybe that's to be expected," she whispered to herself. In a way though, winter break was just what the doctor ordered. Jake seemed happier, and he all but destroyed every snowdrift on the block. Still, she wondered what the situation with her father, called Opa by the kids, would do to him.

Mark Fralick

4

SNOW SNAKES

The night had been cold and snowy; the day hadn't warmed much. A new blanket of snow, light and fluffy, blew about in the brisk breeze. The sun, now beginning to fade, cast shades of pink and orange on the horizon.

Like many homes in his neighborhood, Jake's house sat near the front of the property, with a small garage in the rear. Jake eyed the long shadows of the trees that surrounded his house. The dark silhouettes from the oak trees, turning long and narrow, became strangely distorted this late in the day. Shadows reached up snow banks and back down, filling odd niches made by blowing snow and the occasional snowball.

Jake loved these old oaks. For the biggest of these, an old Black Oak situated in the center of his back yard, he had a name. He figured that something so grand and old had to be called something. Then one day, while listening to the radio, Jake heard it. The announcer was talking about a famous singer.

Sometimes they used his name - sometimes they just called him the *King*. Well, if any tree was the *King*, it was this one.

Jake named this tree Elvis. Elvis had gigantic branches. Some were as big as Jake's waist, not just the lower branches either, but the really high ones too. Jake figured this tree must be about a thousand years old. Well, at least a couple hundred anyway. This was some tree all right. He could climb just a few branches into Elvis's *arms* and just about disappear.

The tree embraced him. It hid and protected him. Elvis gave him a place to go when he didn't want to be anywhere at all.

Shhh, Jake heard, as the wind rustled through Elvis's branches. As some oaks do, Elvis kept many of his leaves during the winter, brown and crackly though they were. Jake loved that sound.

Shhhhh, a bit longer now, as another gust came up. He smiled, finding comfort in the sound. Jake had waded through the snow and jumped from their snow-covered picnic table onto Elvis's first set of branches. He sat quietly... listening.

"Jake, time to go!" he heard his mom announce from below. "The old man is really talking up a storm tonight!" she said about Elvis, as she started to clear snow from the car.

"Alright Elvis, got to go!" Jake said, hanging from one of Elvis's thick arms. *Shhhh*, was Elvis's only response as Jake dropped into a large snowdrift below. Brushing off and walking to the car, the fresh snow squeaked beneath his boots.

"Jake, help your sister in, would you?" Jake's mom

asked.

"Come on Em." Jake said, as he helped her into her car seat. His mother had a habit of over-dressing Emily for the cold weather.

"Ah," he whispered, "you can hardly move."

Dressed in one of Jake's old snowsuits, Emily could barely move her little arms. Quick to laugh and to cry, she giggled as Jake lifted her into the back seat and buckled her in.

Emily, her blond curls bouncing about her expressive face, began singing the *Wheels on the Bus* song. Closing the back door to the car, Jake hopped into the front seat next to his mom.

As dusk settled in, they were off to the airport.

"Another one!" Jake called.

"Nudder one!" Emily echoed from the back seat.

Jake was spotting *snow snakes*. Snow snakes, as they called them, could only be seen from cars and were best spotted at night.

As their car sped along the freshly plowed roads, crosswinds pushed the fresh, flying snow in just such a way to create squiggly lines that danced across the road for only seconds at a time. The car's headlights brought these elusive snow snakes to life.

"There's one," Jake's mom observed a moment later. Julia was not new to this. Many years ago, her father came up with this game to keep her occupied on the drive home from school.

"Yep, that's six," Jake agreed.

"Seven!" A voice replied from the darkness of the back seat. From her vantage point, buckled in the back seat, Emily had never actually seen one of these. She just liked to count along.

"No Em - that was six."

"Eight... nine," she continued.

"Em!" Jake called.

"Ten, 'leben'..." she responded.

"Emmmiiilllyyyy! We aren't doing counting now!" Jake complained while their mom smiled.

There was silence for a moment. "Welve!" Emily blurted confidently from the darkness of the back seat, as if to prove her point. That was enough to get Jake laughing as their car entered the brightly lit entrance to the airport. They parked and headed into the terminal.

5

ARRIVALS

The automatic doors of the airport terminal whisked opened as the three approached. Warm air rushed toward them as they made their way through the doorway. A huge open space lie ahead of them. Jake stared for a second, eyeing the huge designs above them.

"Paper airplanes!" Jake marveled, stashing his hat and gloves into his jacket pockets. Perhaps thirty feet above them hung a display of giant paper airplanes. They were big, colorful, and of all sizes. Some of them had to be as long as twenty feet. Long like a knife but with a small wingspan, most of these planes looked like the classic type that Jake typically made.

One or two of the airplanes had a different design, with shorter, wider, double-fold wings. These weren't too unlike the *Stealth Fighter* model he had at home. Jake knew how to make this type of paper airplane, but he could never get them to fly very well. 'Wings too floppy,' he thought to himself.

"Shine 'em up!" he heard from a distance, drawing Jake's attention to the people in the terminal. There he saw people of all kinds; business people, what he figured to be college kids, and families.

Most of them seemed to have a very good idea of where they were going. Jake, however, did not. "Shine 'em up!" he heard again.

"We need to look at a monitor," he heard from behind him. Jake's mom, holding Emily's hand, quickly caught up. "Over there," she pointed. They walked toward the bank of gray TV screens.

Across from the display screens, a man stood next to a big wooden chair. The odd looking chair, with its wooden seat, big brass arms and steps, did not look very comfortable. But, it seemed to Jake that if you sat in this thing you'd be about six feet high.

"Shine 'em up! Have some time, get a shine!" called the man standing next to the chair. He had the word *Marvin* stitched onto his shirt and called out to no one in particular.

"Sssine um up!" Emily agreed, standing next to Jake. A small man with a big personality, Marvin looked over at Emily and smiled a huge smile at her. Marvin's bright eyes and graying mustache lie in contrast to his dark skin. But the thing Jake noticed most about this man was his smile. Among his very white teeth was a single gold tooth.

A tall man dressed in a suit stopped and stepped up into the big chair.

"Oh, now these are some *fine* shoes," they heard Marvin comment as he began to apply some goopy looking paste.

"I'll make 'em look new again mister, I guarantee

it," Marvin said, smiling.

"I always say I'd rather put a five dollar shine on some fine shoes like these than a twenty-five dollar shine on a five dollar pair. But either way they'll look brand new!" Marvin continued.

Marvin was a talker all right, and he played those shoes like a drummer. A small cloth snapped a beat, matching the music coming from Marvin's small radio. The man in the suit watched on. Captivated by the sharp, rhythmic movement of Marvin's hands, Jake barely heard his mother calling for him to keep up.

"Gate 23...this way," their mom said, as she got her bearings. Together they walked toward the big black sign over the area where the airplanes came and went. Northwest, Pan Am, Delta, United - an odd combination of words Jake observed, while reading the big sign. Many people waited beneath it as travelers came and went.

Jake surveyed the people standing outside the entrance. Families mostly, he figured. Some looked excited, waiting for their mom or dad to come back home, he supposed. Others seemed very sad as they kissed a parent or grandparent goodbye. Still others, he observed, just looked tired.

"Here he comes," Julia said, after several minutes.

"Comes Opa!" Emily squeaked with excitement.

Opa, a tall man with small patches of pure white hair set tight against the sides of his head, made his way up the ramp. His gaze, clear and bright, gave no hint of his age. His walk was steady, though he used a plain wooden cane for support.

Her boy has his grandfather's eyes, Jake's mom often

thought. That half-squint, she surmised, always telling her he was up to some type of mischief.

"Emmy!" he called, as he approached. With that, Emily broke from her mother's grip, skillfully dodged other travelers, and leapt into her grandfather's arms.

"Weeee," he exclaimed, as he hooked his cane on his arm, lifted Emily from her feet, and spun her in circles.

Looking down at Jake with Emily in his arms, Opa took measure of his grandson. "Jake, my lad, you've outdone yourself. You've got to be a foot taller than last time."

It had only been a couple months since Opa had closed up his cabin in northern Wisconsin and made his annual migration south for the winter.

"Come give me a hug," he continued. Jake didn't need a second invitation. He grabbed his grandfather around the waist and gave a big squeeze.

"Hi Daddy," Jake's mom said, after kissing her father on the cheek. Digging around in her grandfather's jacket pockets, searching for treats she knew she'd find, Emily beamed. Together the four of them made their way to the escalator.

Mark Fralick

6

THE FIRST LESSON

Gliding down the escalator, Jake saw a man in a uniform ahead of them. "Cool, a soldier," he said. "It must be cool to be able to shoot guns and toss grenades! Maybe I could do stuff like that when I'm a grown-up man."

"Jacob! First of all, that man is a Marine," Opa said firmly. Jake glanced at his mom, who gave him a look as if to say *oops, now you've done it.*

Opa continued the lesson, "Secondly, the ability to bring harm to others does not make you a man. A truer measure of a man would be to possess the *ability* to use force, but then make the choice, whenever possible, *not* to do so. And I certainly think it takes a lot more than guns and grenades to make a Marine. I talked to that man on the plane and I think he would tell you the same."

They were at the bottom of the escalator when Opa called out, "Gunnery Sergeant?"

"Yes, Sir!" came the response. Jake had somehow forgotten that his grandfather had been a Commander in the Navy. He had served as an engineer in the legendary Sea Bees a long time ago - in a, now, mostly forgotten war. The Sea Bees are the U.S. Navy's Construction Battalion.

Jake loved the Sea Bees mascot, a very determined and angry looking bee, carrying both construction tools and a machine gun.

Jake's grandfather, one of the original officers of this unique group of fighting engineers, still felt a strong connection to anyone serving in the Armed Forces. Jake only now fully understood his mom's warning glare from a few minutes ago.

"What can I do for you, Commander?" the Marine continued.

"Gunny, I'd like you to meet my grandson, Jake," Opa said.

Jake, now keenly aware of what he was *in for* - politely held his hand out and said, "Good to meet you, Gunnery Sergeant!"

Jake knew, full well, how to address a member of the military, especially with his grandfather nearby. While it was okay for his grandfather, a veteran, to use the word *Gunny*, the nickname for this man's rank, it was not so for Jake. He knew the only way for him to address a member of the military was by their full rank, if he knew it, or by the word *Sir* or *Ma'am*. No exceptions...ever.

"Well, young man," the Marine smiled, "it's nice to meet you too. My name is Gunnery Sergeant Owens."

Sergeant Owens was a big man in all respects. Taller even than Jake's grandfather, his arms were thick and shoulders huge. Yes, this man was a mountain. "I think you know my nephew, Lay," he said, as he pointed to a boy around Jake's age.

"Hey Lay," Jake said.

"Hey Jake," Lay said with a big smile. Layton Owens was one of the really smart boys in school. He was shorter than Jake was and thin. Like his uncle, Lay had darker skin than Jake. He wore round-rimmed glasses and just, well, *looked* smart. Lay seemed quite nice, though Jake didn't know him well.

"Gunnery Sergeant," Opa started, "please tell young Jacob something. What are the most important weapons of the Marine Corps?"

"Yes, Commander," said the Sergeant, with no hint of hesitation. "I would say our major weapons are our code, our tactics and our training. The chief article of our code reads *I will never forget that I am an American, fighting for freedom, responsible for my actions, and dedicated to the principles which made my country free.*"

"What about other weapons?"

"Yes Sir," the Marine continued, "as you know, *we* are professionals. It is our tactics, logistics, and training that separate us from other, less prepared and disciplined, forces. We will use force when it is called for - but use it only within the guidelines provided for by our command. That said, when we are called to do so, our tactics, training, aggressiveness and commitment to our country make us formidable foes. You do *not* want to be an enemy of the United States Marine Corps!"

"Thank you, Gunnery Sergeant."

"No problem, Commander!"

Jake's grandfather, a retired engineer and teacher, never passed up an opportunity to teach *life lessons*. Jake smiled at his mom as they both wondered if they should really be surprised that Opa got his first lesson in before they even left the airport.

7

THE GAME

The trip home added four more *snow snakes* to the toll started by Jake on the way to the airport. Jake had spotted three; his grandfather got the last one.

"Jake, would you help with the luggage?" his mother asked, as she brought the car to rest in their driveway. Together, Jake and his grandfather managed the bags while his mom carried a sleeping Emily into the house. "Got everything?" she asked the men.

"We have everything in hand, don't you worry," came the rhythmic response from her father. "Jacob and I just aren't in a hurry," he finished, as they got to the doorway.

Jake noticed a funny look on his mother's face as she held open the door. She squinted just slightly and pressed her lips together. He'd seen this look before all right. It was her *just what is going on here* look. Then, slowly a tiny smile appeared on her face. "Well, let me close the door and shut out cold; it's going to be freezing and windy, I'm told." she responded.

Jake's grandfather looked at his daughter for a

moment with that same half-smile and let out a small grunt.

The four took off their coats in the living room. With a roomy living room and kitchen on the first floor, all three bedrooms of Jake's home were up stairs.

"Come on up Opa, you're staying in my room," Jake interrupted. "Wait 'til you see all the models I've done. Two battleships, the *Missouri* and the *Wisconsin*, and a *Tomcat*!" The *Tomcat* referred to the *F-14* fighter jet that Jake thought looked really cool.

Jake loved building these models. But, it wasn't just that he liked to figure out how things went together; it was imagining how it might have been to see these things in real life – like Opa had.

"Okay, my boy, show me the way," Opa nodded, "it's very nice of you to welcome my stay." With that, the two of them made their way upstairs to Jake's room.

"Hmmm" Julia said softly, watching the two *men* move her father's bags upstairs. Looking at Emily, now asleep on the couch, "Time to get to bed; you big old sleepy head," she whispered. "Oh my, he's got me doing it too…," she said with a chuckle, as she carefully picked up Emily and headed upstairs.

Jake and his grandfather surveyed the new additions to the collection. Models were everywhere in Jake's room. Many of the airplanes and jets hung from the ceiling by fishing line or thread. Some of these were involved in *dogfights* or complicated formations. Others were just flying off by themselves.

The ships were in places of honor on his desk and

bookshelves. There were battleships - these were Jake's favorite, destroyers, old *PT* boats and one aircraft carrier. That carrier had taken Jake a month to build. *Way too many parts*, he decided while building it. It would be the first and last carrier he'd ever build.

"Jake, these models are quite nicely done; judging from the look of them, they must have been fun!"

"Opa, did you know you just rhymed?"

"Did I now? Did I now? Well, I'm quite sure I don't know how," his grandfather said with a knowing smile.

"Yep, and maybe downstairs, too," as Jake thought about it.

"Are you sure, have you listened that well? I wasn't sure how long we'd go before you could tell!" his grandfather finished.

"Well, I thought I heard you rhyme downstairs, but I thought it was on accident."

"Just a little game your mom and I would play; maybe you and I can try it another day. But now I'm tired, it's time for a bit of a rest; because even grown-ups need sleep to be at their best."

With that, Jake headed off to join Emily for bed. Emily's room, just down the hall, was on the other side of the bathroom shared by all the rooms upstairs. "Mom?" he asked, as he saw his mother putting his little sister to bed.

"Yes, dear?"

"Tell me about the rhyming game."

"You noticed," she said, as she sat down beside him on the bed. "I wasn't sure if you would. Your Opa believes you can tell a lot about a person by their vocabulary and how they make their point in a conversation. You know what the word 'vocabulary' means don't you?"

"Words, right?" Jake suggested.

"Yes, words," she nodded. "Your Opa believes that the kinds of words you use are a direct reflection of your education and upbringing. Well, a long time ago your Opa decided I needed to increase my vocabulary and my diction, which is about how you choose and pronounce words. So, we started this game where we talk to each other in rhymes. The first person that can't carry on the conversation loses. He's very good at it."

"That sounds like a really hard game. He said he would play it with me sometime. I probably could never win," Jake observed.

"Well, if you get into a game with your Opa," his mother warned, "you will have to work hard to win. You'll need to pay close attention to what he's saying because one of the rules is that you have to *be in* the conversation. Just saying some rhyme that has nothing to do with what you are talking about doesn't count. Watch out for that one, it tripped me up a lot."

"Did it take you a long, long time to get good at it?"

"Not so long, start with ending your sentences with easy words to rhyme. Use short words that end in a long vowel sound, like *no* or *may*. Eventually, he won't give you credit for easy rhymes, but you can probably start out that way."

"Ok" Jake said, looking forward to the challenge.

"Time to go to bed now, mister; but please be sure not to wake your sister," his Mother said with a smile.

Awkwardly, and after a long pause, he responded,

"Okay, um, okay, I won't make a peep; I'll get ready and then go to sleep."

His mother smiled as she closed the bedroom door.

Mark Fralick

8

SLEDDING AND SLIDING

The final days of winter break passed quickly. Soon Jake would be back in school.

"Zoooom!" Opa yelled from the sled, as it shot down the hill.

"Zoooom!" Emily agreed, perched on her grandfather's lap.

The neighborhood's sledding hill sat on a vacant lot very near Jake's house. This part of the city lies just on the edge of the *valley* of Milwaukee. The valley and the Milwaukee River were the low points of the area. Jake's block sits along the northern most rim of the valley.

The sledding hill, called *Hirsch's Hill* by the kids in the neighborhood, had never been built upon. Its long sweeping slope and absence of trees made it a great spot for sledding. A sidewalk ran along the entire width of the lot only feet from the start of the hill.

For more than a generation, families came from blocks away to sled on Mrs. Hirsch's hill. Actually, this wasn't Mrs. Hirsch's property at all, but since her house was at the bottom of the long hill, the name stuck.

Jake thought Mrs. Hirsch was a nice enough woman. Often, she would come out during nice days with miniature red marker cones. Watching from her deck, she would walk out to where the kids' sleds stopped and mark the one that made it the furthest. Those days were great fun for the kids. Yes, she was nice enough. Jake just thought she looked odd.

Well, really, it was her hair. She had blue-grey hair to start with. 'Just doesn't look real,' Jake couldn't help thinking whenever he saw her. "Who has blue hair?" he would sometimes mumble to himself when he saw her.

But to top it off, her hair didn't, to Jake's eyes, seem quite *attached* to her head. Instead, it appeared to him more like some kind of *hair helmet* that just seemed to hover over her head. Whenever Jake saw her, it was difficult for him to take his eyes off that hair.

But Opa always insisted Jake use very special manners around Mrs. Hirsch. "She is a true survivor," Opa pointed out to Jake.

"You see, there are victims and there are survivors in this world. Many people become victims of horrible deeds or situations through no doing of their own. It is terrible, there can be no question. But some people never recover or, worse, become defined by it. These people are forever victims.

"Now, Mrs. Hirsch was a victim of incredible hatred. These horrible people even marked her with a number. But she is not defined by this brutality, nor does she live life as a victim.

"Resilience, maybe the most important trait of the human spirit, defines her - not the villainy and evil she survived. She's raised a great family in this area and is always there to enjoy the kids of the neighborhood."

Mrs. Hirsch, sitting on an old lawn chair on a snow-cleared portion of her deck, smiled as she watched the proceedings.

"I'm going to beat you!" yelled Jake, not far behind Opa and Emily.

The only real way to sled in this family was on their *old-fashioned* wooden sleds with painted metal rails. Either these sleds or real wood toboggans were the only way to go. None of these cheap plastic sheets some of the other kids used.

Opa kept these old sleds in peak condition over the years. Every spring he'd sand the rust from the rails and paint them bright red. Classic old sleds were these, and fast.

Jake's mom surveyed her family. The three of them had snow in every possible seam of their clothes. "Honestly," she said to herself, "I'm not sure who is worse – the kids or my father!"

"Dad, don't over-do it," she warned. 'As if it will do any good,' she thought to herself.

"Oh, it's way too late for that, my dear," was Opa's only response. Dressed in a sturdy old wool coat, heavy leather gloves and his trusty walking cap, he positioned the sled for another run.

Emily, clad in one of Jake's old hooded snowsuits, leapt into Opa's lap.

"Yep," Opa once explained to Jake, "you can steer these old sleds. It's not like heading down the hill *willy-nilly*, not knowing what you're going to crash in to. These babies are built for speed but you're never out of control."

Emily and Opa sped down the hill, faster than ever. Jake followed.

"Woo! Look at that old sled Jake has to use. Poor little Jakey!" came an unfriendly voice. It was Jimmy Melder. Jimmy, clutching a molded plastic sled, faked agony on his face to bring the point home.

"Jimmy Melder!" Jake said to himself as he, his sister and grandfather made it back to the top of the hill.

Jake's mom watched on. Jimmy was much taller than Jake, with a slim and lanky build. He seemed to have grown beyond his years. She knew, very well, the situation with this boy. Jimmy was the neighborhood bully.

Jimmy and Jake grew up on this block together and were, at one time, fast friends. But something happens to some boys when they mature faster than others. She wished she understood it. How did a nice little boy turn into this big old bully?

"James! James Melder, is that you?" Jake's grandfather called, as he stomped the snow from his boots. "A shiny piece of plastic you have there. Is it new?" he asked, not calling it a sled.

"Yep, got it for Christmas" Jimmy smiled proudly, his curly red hair peeking out beneath his black *49ers* hat.

"You've noticed Jake's sled is from the past, but I'm sure your sled doesn't go as fast." Opa continued.

'Oh great,' Jake thought. 'This is all I need.' Jake's usual strategy for Jimmy was to ignore him. One of Opa's favorite sayings comes from the lyrics of a song, *Confront your enemies, avoid them when you can.* Jake usually opted for avoidance; Opa was more likely to choose confrontation.

"A race?" Jimmy asked, grinning wildly. "I'll kick his butt! Let's go to Mrs. Hirsch's poles," talking about the clothes line poles, well past the bottom of the hill.

"Well now, James, I'm not sure where you got that language, but all of that remains to be seen - doesn't it?" Jake's grandfather's face instantly turned from that of the big old kid, racing down the hill, to that of a wise old teacher.

Opa turned to Jake and spoke in a voice only he could hear. "Remember what I taught you about how these old sleds work?"

"Yep," Jake said in a low voice. "The rails cause just a little bit of ice to melt underneath them, making things much more slippery. It makes them fastest on packed snow or ice."

"What about Jimmy's sled?" Opa asked.

"Jimmy's sled will be faster on unpacked snow," Jake answered.

"Use what you know," Opa said to Jake, as he turned back to Jimmy. "Alright, Mr. Melder, you think that shiny piece of plastic is faster than one of my old relics, do you? Well, we shall see." With that, he led Jake over to a spot from which both he and Jimmy could start.

"What do you know?" Opa said quietly.

"I know that I need to stay on the icy part of the hill in order to go fastest. I know that I can control my direction but Jimmy probably can't. And I know I just don't like that Jimmy very much and wish you hadn't gotten me into this," Jake said, not looking very happy.

"Sorry about that my lad, maybe my mistake," Opa continued. "I'm sure it will be...hmmm. Jake, do you know what the word yield means?" Opa asked.

"It's like to stop, right?" Jake responded.

"Well, almost." Jake's grandfather said, whispering now. "It is really more like to *give way* or to let the other guy go first. Sometimes you must decide when to stand and when it's time to yield..."

"Remember that some people need to win, for it's their ego it feeds; so in the end, you need to recognize it's just what the other guy needs."

"Like it's more important to him than to me?" Jake asked, as he positioned himself on the sled. "Well, I guess we'll just have to see..." not saying that he'd really, really like to beat Jimmy.

Both of them smiled.

Jimmy got himself set next to Jake.

"Ready...Set...Go" Opa called.

Cheers rang out from all the other kids on the hill, as the race started. Jimmy got off to a fast start. His friends, the other *junior bullies*, screamed wildly. Jake was not far behind him - not catching up, but not losing ground either.

Then Jake steered his sled over a few feet, onto the big patch of ice he'd been sliding on all day. He immediately shot forward.

"Oooh!" was the crowd's reaction to this maneuver, then excited screams. The rest of the kids on the hill now drowned out the yells of Jimmy's friends.

At this point, however, Jimmy leaned sideways on his plastic *sled*, pushing his arms down against its flimsy sides. Having only meager steering abilities, he leaned over so far that his sled nearly rolled. Jimmy's efforts paid off. He managed to shift his course enough to move onto the faster snow. Jimmy picked up speed, gaining some of the distance that he'd lost to Jake.

Now, neck and neck, they sped down the hill, separated only by inches. Seeing Jimmy catch up, Jake leaned forward trying to get an edge.

Having melted a bit and refrozen, the bottom portion of the hill had become very icy the later part of the afternoon. This played into Jake's hands, as his sled was much faster on ice. He began to distance himself from Jimmy.

Looking back at Jimmy, now leaning forward as much as he could, Jake saw the grimace on his face. At that, Jake smiled, letting Jimmy see him smile. He also let Jimmy, and only Jimmy, see him ever so slightly press his heels against the icy snow. The added friction allowed Jimmy to catch up.

By now, everyone on the hill was yelling for one

boy or the other. As they got to the makeshift *finish line*, the boys ended up in a dead heat. Everyone on the hill seemed happy with the outcome. After a moment, the others went back to sledding and sliding.

Jimmy looked at Jake with a sideways glance as Jake said, "I just caught a lucky break and since it could have gone either way, a tie seemed like the right thing."

Jimmy seemed a bit perplexed by the whole thing. But as his friends sped down the hill on their new plastic *sleds*, Jimmy lifted his arms above his head and yelled "WoooHooo!" He celebrated as the victor as his friends popped up off their rides.

As Jimmy and his friends walked up the hill for another run, he glanced back at Jake and gave him just a touch of a nod.

Getting ready to call it a day, Jake's mother, sister and grandfather gathered around him.

"That was quite a run, honey," Jake's mother said, as she brushed some of the snow from his jacket.

"I don't know, I think I need to check that sled's rail slides; it looked to me like toward the end it just up and died," Opa said, in a half-smile.

"Sometimes having more than one winner is okay, I'm sure there will be other chances on some other day," Jake said thoughtfully.

"Well said and very well done, my clever young grandson," Opa said encouragingly. Julia laughed at that.

"Cold!" was Emily's response to all of this talk.

"Okay, sweetheart. Time for dinner soon anyway," her mother said, as she leaned down and kissed Emily's very red nose.

9

THE BIG BOOTH

Opa loved to eat out. He loved all kinds of different food, but pizza was his favorite. It happened that the family's favorite pizza place was just around the corner from their house. "Michael's" it was called or "Mike's" to everyone in the neighborhood. Not a very Italian sounding name, but the pizza was the best around.

Mike's was kind of a dark place with brown wood-paneled walls. Red light poured off the big neon *Michael's* sign into the front window. This further darkened the look of the place.

A dozen or so tables, with red and white-checkered tablecloths, filled the main room, flanked by three big red vinyl booths. Jake liked the booths because you could really spread out. Especially the one in the corner, you could probably fit about 10 kids in there, he figured.

Tonight the plan was to meet Gunnery Sergeant Owens and some of his family for the pizza buffet. Mike's only did the buffet once a week, on

Wednesday nights.

While rare for the kids to eat out on a weeknight, Jakes's Mom knew that Gunny Owens would be reporting back to duty soon. He and Opa became quite good friends during his leave and she wanted to make sure Opa got one last chance to see him.

Plus, kids only had to pay twice their weight in pennies on *Buffet Night*. For that kind of deal, costing her all of two dollars to feed both Jake and Emily, their mom couldn't pass it up.

Arriving a little early, Jake's mom let Mike know there would be seven of them for dinner. Mike's head spun around, as he quickly surveyed the open tables.

Jake held his breath as Mike pointed, almost as if in slow motion. "How about the big booth?" Mike asked.

"Yes!" Jake whispered emphatically, as he happily punched the air. 'Tonight must be our lucky night – the big booth,' he thought, as they made their way between the tables to the big corner booth.

They got themselves situated in the booth as Mike brought over four waters. "We'll wait for our friends," Jake's mother said.

"Just help yourselves whenever you're ready," Mike said politely, as he headed back to the kitchen.

"I'm going to have a sausage and a pepperoni and maybe just a cheese," Jake mused.

"Let's make sure our eyes aren't bigger than our stomach, mister," came the usual warning from his mother.

"He got big tomach!" assured Emily, pointing at her brother's midsection.

The three of them laughed. A distracted Opa did not. He looked upset. Jake realized that the people in the booth next to them were being very loud. They called the waitress, a very nice woman with dark skin, a bad name.

In Jake's house, this particular word was possibly the worst thing anyone could ever say. The waitress looked stunned and upset.

"I would say that is quite enough." Opa said as he stood, not bothering with his cane.

"Be careful, Daddy," Jake's mom said to her father's deaf ears.

"Well now," Jake's grandfather said in a very firm voice, looking down at the men seated in the neighboring booth. "I'm wondering what kind of men you are."

"Sit down, old man!" one of them said, his mouth half full of pizza.

"It would seem to me," Jake's grandfather continued a bit louder now, "that there are only two types of people that would use such an ugly word. First, there are those with hatred in their puny little hearts. They use that kind of language to hurt people. It makes them feel superior. You see, they have to do something to make themselves feel big because they hate the fact that they are so small and insignificant."

Opa's face had turned from that of a kind old man to that of someone on a deadly serious mission. His eyes, fixed steadily on the men, flashed sharp as a knife.

"And second," he continued, "are those who are so ignorant that they don't realize the pain they are causing with that foul word." After a long pause, he asked, "My question is simple. Which are you?"

"We are going to have a serious problem!" one of them said as he started to stand.

"That would be a mistake," came a calm but somehow threatening voice from behind Jake's grandfather.

It was Gunny Owens, with Lay and Lay's mom in tow. He glanced at Jake's grandfather and continued. "This man is a retired officer of the United States Navy. I am a Marine. He served so the likes of you would have the right to be free. He should have your respect. I would not attempt to harm him if I were you."

He had the fearless look of a professional warrior. Even Jake was shaken by his gaze, made even more menacing by the dark lighting of Mike's.

The men looked at each other, as if considering their options.

"It's time for you to leave!" another voice added. It was Mr. Melder, Jimmy's dad, now standing next to Gunny Owens.

Around the restaurant you could hear the chairs loudly sliding as men stood in support. It became very quiet. The three men at the table suddenly felt very alone.

"You go now," said Mike, emerging from his kitchen. "Don't want your money. Just leave!"

The three thought better of the situation. One of them took a last drink from his glass, slammed it down, and got up. He mumbled something to his friends and all three left with no other words.

Everyone in Mike's cheered.

"Thank you," said the waitress, as she brought over three more glasses of water. "Anything else to drink?"

"You're welcome, but I feel like I have to appologize for those people," Opa said, his eyes now soft and sincere. "We'll have three small Sprites and four Cokes please. They had no business using that kind of unforgivable language. I feel awful."

"Sir," she said, "it's not the first time I've been called a name, and I'm sure it won't be the last. I don't blame you, your family or anyone else the same color as you. They don't know me. They just get their kicks from judging me by my color. Wouldn't I be a fool if I judged others the same way? I'll have those drinks right up. Help yourself to the buffet."

"Well isn't that amazing..." Opa said thoughtfully. "Here is a woman who has hatred thrown in her face, but refuses to hate in return. That's a lesson for all of us."

Opa glanced over to the Melder's table and gave a thankful nod to Mr. Melder, who nodded seriously in reply. Jimmy had seen the whole thing and shot a smile to Jake and Lay. They smiled back.

"Well, she's a bigger person than I'd have been," Gunny Owens offered.

"I'm sorry Gunnery Sergeant, *no one* is a bigger person than you," Jake slid into the conversation.

Laughter... finally!

Later, after everyone had as much sausage and pepperoni as they could handle, Jake asked, "Opa, why did you do that before, weren't you scared?"

Lay looked up, interested in the answer.

"Well, what are my three rules?" Opa asked.

"Don't be a fool. Don't follow fools. And, always do the right thing." Jake said. He knew these well.

"So, where would you put this?" Jake's grandfather asked, now talking to both the boys.

"I'd say *doing the right thing*," Lay said.

"Yep," Jake agreed.

"You know, what's funny about doing the right thing is this: Sometimes when you need most to do it, it means doing something that is difficult or something that may not be the best for *you* personally. I try always to do the right thing, especially when it is not the easiest thing to do. You see, to me *doing the right thing* defines us as men."

"But what if it is dangerous?" came a boy's voice from behind them. It was Jimmy Melder.

"Hello there young James, good to see you again," Jake's grandfather said. "Come here and chat with us. Well, James, that's all about courage. Sometimes we must find the courage to do the right thing. Now Jake, courage isn't about not being afraid, is it?"

"Nope, its when you may be afraid of something, but you do what you need to do anyway," came Jake's response. Jake and his grandfather had many talks about courage, so he knew the answer to this one, too.

"Yes," Opa smiled. "You see, courage is maybe the most important quality of a man. If you don't have courage, you can't have any other qualities that really matter...for very long anyway. Without courage, you'll be teased or intimidated into submitting to someone else's way or perhaps even changing altogether."

After a long pause, Opa continued thoughtfully. "Now, I've known men of great courage in my time and don't count myself as one of them. Even though

I felt afraid of those three men, I knew that they and everyone in this room needed to know that what they were doing...was wrong. So, I decided the right thing to do was confront those men."

"I believed that if I got into trouble, there would be others that might help. You see, people are drawn to courage. Courage compells courage in others. So sometimes, all it takes is a good example for others to find the courage within themselves. I was hoping. Anyway, who would hurt a defensless old man like me?" Opa said with a wink.

"There are lots of people who would beat you up, even if you're old," came Jimmy's response. After a second or so he added "or even kids like us."

To the other boys Jimmy didn't now seem so big and so bad. In that moment he just seemed kind of sad in a way.

"Yes, my young friends, there are bad people in this world. Hopefully not *lots* though. They come in all colors and from all over. That's why the good guys have to stick together." Opa continued, looking directly at Jimmy now and smiling.

Jimmy looked at Jake's grandfather for a moment thoughfully, but said nothing. "See you guys," he said, and turned to join his father, who'd been paying their bill at the cash register.

"See ya, Jimmy," Lay said.

"Yeah, see ya," Jake added.

Mark Fralick

10

SCHOOL TIME

With winter vacation behind them, the long stretch of school days until spring break began. Jake did not look forward to this part of the year. Sure, there were a couple of one-day holidays, but nothing like a whole week off or anything fun like that. So, time moved slowly for all the kids at Silverbrook Intermediate School during this time of the year, especially for Jake.

Mrs. Jackson's math class was maybe the most difficult for Jake. Most of the kids thought her class was the hardest. She was a tough teacher, but usually wore a smile to go along with the brightly colored dresses for which she was known.

Though not a tall woman, Mrs. Jackson commanded attention when she entered a room. It may have been those dresses of hers, or her large, fluffy body. However, Jake thought it was probably her eyes. She possessed the eyes of a brilliant mind, and they could see right through you. She was loud and tough, but also very funny.

Mrs. Jackson had a habit of launching a blackboard eraser at you if she thought you were not *in the game*. Yes, you needed to be on your toes in this class. Many a kid left that class with an embarrassing rectangular shaped imprint temporarily etched into their noggin in chalk dust.

Right now, the class focused on multiplication and division. Not only was the class hard for Jake, but Mrs. Jackson also made the class take timed tests nearly every day. Jake just wasn't very good at working fast; the timed test were especially tough for him.

Lately, to make things worse, Mrs. Jackson started what she called *shoot-outs*. In a shoot-out, two or three kids would stand up in front of the class with a piece of chalk in their hand. She'd then blurt out a problem. The students would then spin around and write the answer on the chalkboard. The first to write the correct answer and underline it, wins.

All of this made for nerve-wracking math classes for Jake.

For Layton Owens it was a very different story. Nearly perfect on every timed test and *deadly* in the shootout, no one ever wanted to go up against him. Lay often began writing the answer before Mrs. Jackson even finished asking the question. Jake, and all of his class, considered Lay the smartest kid in school.

"It would seem to me," Opa began, after hearing this one day, "that your friend may be able to help you. He seems very good at math, and may be able to share something with you. Jake, don't ever believe you need to automatically know everything or be the best, or even good, at something. Everyone has their skills."

"I don't seem to have any," Jake said sadly.

"Well, my boy let me tell you this," Opa continued. "You've got magic in you. I believe everyone has some special, magical thing that they can do. Maybe Lay's magic is math. Maybe yours is something else.

"That's why your mother thinks it's so important for you to try different things - like soccer, softball, and piano. Who knows where you'll find your magic."

"What's your magic, Opa?"

"I can see things that aren't yet there," Opa said, "and build them. I can look at a piece of ground and see, in my mind, how to build an airfield to fit on it."

"Wow," Jake said, somewhat in awe, "should I know what my magic is yet? When did you find your magical thing?"

"Not until I was in college, it wasn't in a flurry. Anyway, my lad, don't be in such a hurry. It was years and years before it appeared to me. But, I know when you're young - patient is the hardest thing to be," Opa rhymed.

"With math it's easy for you to say," Jake said. "Your grade in math was probably always an A."

Opa smiled. "Ah, but here's a thing that's neat. There are many things to math and some are a treat. There are problems, and questions, and riddles with clues. It will be up to you to see all the cues."

"Mrs. Jackson says that word problems are next, probably another thing that Lay will be best," Jake returned awkwardly, trying to stay in the game.

"I think you could be very good at solving

problems of this kind; you build models and can visualize big things in your mind," Opa said, pointing his finger on Jake's head.

"But models are different from math," Jake replied, not really feeling like playing the game anymore.

"Ah, not so different than you might think," Opa said, tapping his finger gently on his forehead. Here's a little word problem. Say I drew a rectangle that is 10 inches by 12 inches. What is the rectangle's volume?"

"That's too hard, Opa!" Jake complained.

"Okay, remember the wood we stacked yesterday? Well, we stacked it into a shape called a rectangle. That's almost like a square, but not all the sides are the same length. In a rectangle, two sides are one length and the other two sides can have a different length. We stacked the wood, 10 pieces high and 12 pieces long. How many pieces were there?"

"That's simps," Jake said quickly, "One hundred twenty!"

"Hmmm, simple you say – why?"

"You just take 10 times 12".

"So," Opa quizzed, "we created a rectangle that was 10 pieces by 12 pieces. What is its volume?"

"Oh," Jake said slowly. "Volume is like what's in the rectangle. So, 10 pieces times 12 pieces is 120 pieces. And 10 inches times 12 inches is 120…"

"Exactly, your first word problem solved; now has your fear of this dissolved?" asked Opa.

"Hmmm, that was actually kind of cool; but I don't know how simple it will be when I'm doing this in school," Jake retorted.

"Jake, think about the way this problem was

solved; what kind of information and knowledge was involved?"

"Well, I knew the math; isn't that at least half?" Jake asked, hoping that Opa wouldn't notice that math and half didn't actually rhyme.

After a pause, Opa smiled as if to say 'gotcha!' The game was over for now. "Yes, the math was important. But it really is the simplest part of doing a word problem. The harder part is just stating the problem in a way you can understand.

"Remember, when I first asked the question about the rectangle, you didn't have any idea what the answer was. But when I put it in a way you could more easily understand - it was, as you said, 'simps'.

"The difference was that you were able to convert the words into a math problem. You converted the fact that we made a 10 by 12 stack of wood into the multiplication problem: what is 10 times 12?

"In other words, you stated the word problem as a mathematical question. That's the real trick to doing word problems: stating the problem. It seems so simple, but it is true.

"So, the rule for doing word problems is this. State the problem, write the problem, and solve the problem...'Simps'."

"Okay, let me try another one," Jake said, wanting to try his hand at this.

"Let's see," Opa mused. "How about this? I bought a small bag of candy. It has 30 pieces in it. I want to share it equally with both of us and your mother. How many pieces would each of us get?"

"Okay, that's easy too." Jake said quickly. "The problem is 30 divided by 3. That equals 10."

"Yes, indeed my young friend - you are very

much onto it; tomorrow we'll see if Mrs. Jackson gives you a fit."

11

CAPTAINS

"I'd like to put all of you into teams," Mrs. Jackson began the next morning. "But here is your first problem. If I were to put this class into, say, 8 teams, how many boys and girls would be on each team?"

There was silence for a moment as everyone looked about. Mrs. Jackson could see some of her kids starting to count out the students. In the middle of the room, a lone hand was raised. Lay Olson was her first thought. No, sitting next to Lay, it was Jake with his hand up.

"Yes, Jake," she said, almost as a question. She wasn't sure if he was going to answer her question or if he may just need to leave the room.

"Three," is all he said.

"Three?" she said, surprised.

"Three," he repeated.

"How did you get this number so fast, Jake?" she asked, unable to mask the surprise in her voice.

"Well, we have 4 rows of 6 kids in here, which

would be a 4 by 6 rectangle. So, 4 times 6 equals 24. You wanted to make eight teams. Okay, 24 divided by 8 is 3."

"Very good, Jake," she commended him. "You will be a team captain. Come on up here."

Mrs. Jackson picked seven other kids to be captains. Together the eight stood at the front of the class.

"Okay, captains," she continued, "each of you will pick the rest of your team, starting with Jake, then Maddie, and so on, moving toward me. Jake, you may start."

"Lay," Jake said. This was a no-brainer. Lay was, easily, the best student in the class. The rest of the class nodded in approval, probably thinking *Yep, just what I would have done.* Lay smiled, stood, and took a position behind Jake.

"Jill," said Maddie. This would be tough. Madison Franks was pretty smart herself and Jill Dubois was the smartest person next to Lay. Yep, they'd be a tough team. Jill took her position behind Maddie.

The rest of the captains picked their first pick. It was getting close to being Jake's pick again. He began to survey the kids that were left.

His eyes met Jimmy Melder's. Jimmy looked away. Jimmy, usually one of the first picked for games out on the playground, would probably be one of the last to be picked for math teams.

Jake wondered if Mrs. Jackson had somehow thought of this when she came up with the idea of teams. Maybe it was a way of turning the tables on kids always picked first for kickball.

This made Jake think about a conversation he had

with his grandfather shortly after the sledding race with Jimmy. "Opa?" Jake asked, "Why did you think that it would be a good idea to let Jimmy win or tie with me? You said that *sometimes the right thing to do is yield*. Why yield to Jimmy? He's not very nice to me!"

Jake was actually being kind. Jimmy had a habit of being very mean to Jake, Lay and some of the other kids.

Opa had heard all the stories - how Jimmy would make fun of the other kids for being smaller. How he and his friends would lay in wait and ambush them with snowballs, and how he was just not very nice to any of them.

"This is what I believe, my young friend," Opa began. "Many bullies aren't tough, they just pretend. Sometimes they're scared or it's something they're hiding; and they often don't have real friends for their confiding. So, on your sled, in that small token; his hard and nasty shell you just may have broken."

"Jimmy!" Jake said, as he completed his whispered conversation with Lay. They chose Jimmy Melder.

This stirred the class in surprise. Jimmy, relieved not to be the last chosen, rose and stood behind Jake and Lay.

Maddie smiled at them. She thought they'd take Justin Duell. Justin was a pretty smart boy. He probably wasn't picked yet because, having just moved into the area, no one really knew him well.

"Justin," Maddie said, as if talking directly to Jake. 'Ouch,' Jake thought. That only makes things worse. Maddie, Jill, and Justin would be the team to beat.

Jake was happy with his choice just the same. Even the boys that normally hung out with Jimmy, and were supposed to be his friends, passed him by. Jake just felt a bit sorry for him.

Anyway, the choices were made; the teams set.

12

TEAMMATES

"The great thing about working in a team," Opa told the boys, "is that it's not just working together, it's also about learning from each other."

The boys had gotten their first set of word problem assignments from Mrs. Jackson and had met at Jake's house after school.

"That's fine, Commander, but these are going to get really, really hard," said Lay. He used Jake's grandfather's rank as instructed to by his uncle. Lay's uncle had a great deal of respect for this man, and made it very clear to Lay about how he was to address him.

"Lay, please, no one really calls me that anymore," Opa said with a smile. "You may call me Opa or Mr. Clayton. Yes, word problems can be hard. But, you just have to break them down, don't you Jake?"

"Yep, it makes things a lot easier," Jake said comfortably. "The first thing to do is to say the problem."

"Yes," Opa continued. "We call that stating the

problem. We try to state the problem in a way that turns it into a mathematical question, and gets rid of all the *gobbledygook* that doesn't have anything to do with the problem."

"It still sounds hard, Mr. Clayton," said Jimmy. Jimmy was not sure about any of this. First of all, he had been thrown into this group because one of his best friends didn't pick him. That made him mad, but it also didn't really surprise him.

Secondly, he hadn't always been very nice to either of these boys and they weren't really his friends. He was very uncomfortable with the whole thing.

"Well," Opa started, smiling at the boys, "let's just see about that; we'll hear that problem and then we'll chat."

"Come on Opa, be cool," Jake said quickly, not knowing what the other boys would think of this. "They're not family, but kids from school."

"Right you are, my young Jake," Opa's response came. "Right you are - my mistake. Let's hear that first problem then."

Lay looked interested in the conversation that just took place. Jimmy, on the other hand, just looked impatient.

Lay began reading the problem. "Five students bring seven marbles each to school one day. They put the marbles into a basket and leave them overnight. The next day one of them is sick. The teacher wants them to take as many marbles home as possible as long as they all take the same number. How many marbles does each student take? Are there any left over?"

"This is stupid!" Jimmy blurted out, disgusted by

all of this. "Why would a bunch of kids take marbles to school, leave them and take them home the next day?"

"Ah," Opa said patiently. "This is one of the secrets to word problems. Sometimes they make up silly sounding situations. A lot of the time, it's just because the person making up the problem doesn't really care about the story. They're just putting odd facts together to make the problem work.

"But sometimes, really smart word problems are written with extra pieces of information to throw you off the trail. Let's try and state the problem, shall we?"

"Okay," Jake said, already having a pretty good handle on this one. "It's five times seven to start with."

"Yep," Lay agreed. "Then we need to find out how many we can send home with four kids. But, 5 times 7 is 35, and 35 can't be divided by 4."

"Nonsense, young Layton," Jake's grandfather scolded. "Any number is divisible by any other number. Except you can't divide by zero because, well, it just doesn't make any sense.

"In any case, you boys are too used to Mrs. Jackson's high-speed division tests where everything is nice and neat. Nine divided by three is three; twenty-five divided by five is five. In those tests, all the answers are nice whole numbers – we call them *integers*, *round*, or *counting* numbers.

"But when you have a problem like this," he continued, "you've got a couple of decisions to make. Do you have what's called a remainder, or do you have a fraction? A remainder is when you've divided things up as much as you can into whole numbers and have some left over. A fraction is when you have part of a piece and you count it like that.

"It's like the three of you dividing up four pieces of cake. You could each have one, and if you were still hungry, you could split that last piece.

"So, in splitting that last piece, you would each have one-third of a piece of cake. That's a fraction. What you need to decide is if this is an integer and remainder question or a fraction question."

"Well, it would be pretty hard to split a marble," Jimmy said, finding this more interesting than he thought he would.

"Right you are, James," Opa said, his eyes smiling at Jimmy. "So, what do you need to do now?"

"We need to find out how many times thirty-five can be divided equally by four kids." Lay said, thinking out loud. "So, thirty-two divided by four is eight, and thirty-six is more than they have. Everyone can take home eight marbles."

"Then," Jake chirped in, "thirty-five minus thirty-two is three. Three would be left over."

"Ah, not so hard after all, wouldn't you say?" Opa said, congratulating the boys. "I think you could do problems like this all day. The thing that I think is number one, is that this whole team helped to get it done. That's teamwork truly at its best, I'm sure you'll do better than the rest."

"You don't know who else is there still," Lay said, deciding to jump in with a rhyme. "It's not only Maddie, but also Justin and Jill."

Opa, Jake, and Lay smiled for a moment. "Come on you guys," Jimmy said, impatient again. "I have to get home soon." Actually, this wasn't exactly true.

Jimmy just wanted to be done with this so he could play snow-football with his friends.

They all got back to work and made their way through the other problems without any other help from Opa.

Mark Fralick

13

JIMMY'S SURPRISE

The next day in Mrs. Jackson's class, each of the teams had to write their answers on the board. Mrs. Jackson was tough. Not only did you have to put the answer up on the board, but you had to write all of the math you used to get to the answer, too.

Some of the teams didn't have all of the math on the board, or even all the math right. But, two teams got everything right, Maddie's and Jake's.

"Okay, class," Mrs. Jackson began, as she looked at the board, "some of you got this right," referring to the problem with the remainder, "but I'm a little disappointed. Let's talk about division for a moment. Jimmy Melder, which of these numbers can be divided by four?"

She wrote five numbers on the board: 3, 8, 15, 20, and 32.

Jake and Lay smiled at Jimmy, hoping he'd remember what Opa said. Jimmy didn't look happy. He hated answering questions in school, but he especially hated answering them for Mrs. Jackson.

"They all can," Jimmy said timidly, after a long pause.

Many in the class giggled at Jimmy, thinking he was giving a *dumb* answer. He looked even more upset. Jake and Lay smiled.

Mrs. Jackson looked stunned for a few seconds and then, too, began to smile.

"Oh, really?" Mrs. Jackson said. "Would you like to explain this, Mr. Melder?"

"Any number can be divided by any other number except zero," Jimmy said, with a bit more confidence now. "So, all of those numbers can be divided by four. Some of those numbers won't come out even, so you'll have either a fraction or an integer with a remainder."

'Who is this boy?' Mrs. Jackson thought. The classroom sat silent; everyone but Jake and Lay surprised by the answer.

"Who would like to explain what an *integer* is?" Mrs. Jackson asked.

Only three hands were up now - Jake's, Lay's and Jimmy's.

"Jake?" Mrs. Jackson asked, still pretty stunned by all of this.

"Integers are counting numbers - round numbers with no fractions," Jake said, matter-of-factly.

"Okay, we'll call them whole numbers," Mrs. Jackson said, thinking to herself that she couldn't ever remember hearing the word *integer* from anyone younger than a middle-school student. She wouldn't even get to fraction math for another month.

She took the rest of the hour explaining to the class about solving problems involving whole numbers and remainders.

Jimmy didn't remember a day when he felt so good about being in school. Not only did he get a question right, which was rare, but he also managed to surprise Mrs. Jackson, of all people. For Jimmy, this was some day all right!

After math class was over, Mrs. Jackson stopped Jake on the way out of the room. "Jake," she asked, "where did the three of you learn about integers and fractions?"

"My grandfather is living with us for a little while, he was helping us," Jake smiled.

"Help indeed," Mrs. Jackson said. "I'd like to talk to him some time, if you can arrange it."

"Sure," said Jake, "he walks with us to school sometimes."

"Have him stop in, would you?" she asked, walking away.

Mark Fralick

14

DODGEBALL

The early spring days had warmed enough to melt all the snow on the blacktop portion of the school's playground. Today, bright and unseasonably warm, became one of those rare spring days that made Wisconsin feel a bit more like Florida. Jackets came off, sleeves rolled up, and the kids pretended it was summer - for a day anyway.

With the blacktop now free of snow, dozens of red rubber playground balls instantly reappeared from their long winter hibernation. Some of them bounced around in friendly games of 4-square; others flew in ruthless games of dodgeball.

Playground dodgeball, something you grew up really loving or really fearing, punished all but the strongest and fastest kids. In order to do well at dodgeball, you had to throw really hard, be very fast, or catch very well.

Jake could really do none of these things very well. Jimmy Melder, on the other hand, was great at all of them.

Jake heard the teachers and parents talk about dodgeball and how they didn't like it being played at all. They worried about the bigger kids picking on the smaller kids.

Jake agreed with the idea that the bigger kids would *pick off* the smaller kids first because they were easy targets. But he also figured that having the bigger kids playing dodgeball at recess meant that they wouldn't have as much time to bully him and some of his classmates. Plus, he really liked to watch, especially when Jimmy Melder and his friends were playing against the bigger sixth graders.

As Jake watched on, about ten kids began a game with three balls in play. The more balls in play, the more to watch out for. In a frenzy of high velocity action, balls flew everywhere.

"See, in dodgeball," Jake explained to one of the younger kids standing by, "if the ball hits you, and you don't catch it before it hits the ground, you're out. If you catch it, the kid who threw the ball is out.

But there's one special rule. If you are holding a ball, you can use it to deflect a ball coming at you. As long as it just hits the ball you're holding, you're not out."

Sometimes, a couple of the kids on one side would wait until they each got a ball and target one of the kids on the other side. It was difficult enough to dodge a hard-thrown ball to begin with, but trying to get out of the way of two? That was all but impossible. Jake hated being on the receiving end of that.

This was the situation at hand. Two sixth graders

remained on one side and just Jimmy on the other. Each of the three remaining players had a ball in his hand. The sixth graders nodded to each other and targeted Jimmy.

Jimmy was quick and he had a ball to use as a deflector. Just as the two balls came at Jimmy, he moved quickly to one side. This maneuver got him out of the path of one ball. The second, now coming right at him, he deflected easily with the ball he held.

Quickly, he raised his arm, aimed, and picked off the taller of the two remaining opponents. The onlookers, including Jake, cheered loudly.

Now the table was turned. The remaining sixth grader ran to collect the ball Jimmy just used to knock out his friend. But Jimmy collected up both of the balls that were tossed at him. Jimmy stood with one ball in his hand and the other under his opposite arm.

The sixth grader wasn't about to throw his only ball at Jimmy and be totally *unarmed*.

Jimmy's move. He moved closer to his opponent, almost to the *off sides* line, unofficially marked by a couple of red mittens.

Jimmy then made a daring move. He bounced the ball that had been in his hand straight down to the playground pavement. He bounced that ball so hard that it leapt high into the air. Then he switched the other ball from under his arm to his throwing hand and quickly let it fly.

The sixth grader jumped out of the way of that ball, but was now off balance. At that same moment, Jimmy caught the ball he had bounced and within a second had it flying toward his opponent. The sixth grader tried to deflect it with his ball, but Jimmy had gone for a leg shot.

Leg shots were hard to defend, especially against a hard thrown ball. Jimmy, leaping into the air to get some extra momentum on the ball, fired a real missile at this kid. The ball hit him right on the top of his foot as he tried to, both, jump out of the way and reach down to deflect it. There were shouts of support from all the fifth graders as the bell sounded, ending recess.

While a lot of the fifth graders didn't like Jimmy much, it was really something when one of their own beat sixth graders at dodgeball.

15

HUMBLE PI

After school that day, Opa listened to this adventure as recalled by the three young members of his math team. Actually, Jake and Lay described the action in vivid detail as Jimmy smiled and listened.

"And you should have seen how far Jimmy bounced that ball," Jake said, pointing up in the air. "It must have gone ten feet high. Then by the time that other kid knew what happened, Jimmy nailed him with a rocket of a leg shot. It was awesome!"

"Hmmm," Opa said, after a short pause, "it seems to me, young James, that you are very good at this game, but I'd caution you to be careful next time, just the same."

By now, the other two boys were more than used to Opa speaking in rhyme, and even Jimmy rhymed back at him from time to time.

"You see," he continued, "if someone is smart and their brain worth a dime; they'll not make that same mistake the next time. They'll understand that teamwork is better planned sooner rather than late; and as a team, target you early and seal your fate.

Remember, teamwork almost always works best; no matter whether its math or a sport that's your test."

"When the three of you play dodgeball together," Opa continued after a pause, "do you play as a team?"

"We don't play together," Jimmy said, after a long, very uncomfortable, pause.

"Well, why not?" Opa asked, already knowing the answer.

"We aren't really good enough," Lay started, "to play with Jimmy and his friends. They shoot really, really hard. I'm not very good at dodgeball anyway, but Jake isn't too bad."

"Nah, I'm not that good enough either," Jake admitted.

"Sorry," Opa said, faking surprise, "I guess I just assumed you were a team. Okay then, let's talk about pi."

"Pie, like that problem where we had to split a piece of pie? That's too easy," responded Jimmy, happy the subject had changed.

"No, young James," Opa said, smiling. "Pi, spelled *P-I*, is a magic number." Opa paused for a moment to gather his thoughts. "I believe there are wonders in nature, but why they exist - we haven't a clue. You see, they seem too magical, too planned, or too perfect to be true. There are more things like this that you'll find in math and in nature than you can know; each leads me to believe there is a greater power with these hints to show. Someone or something has a plan, you see; there are just too many of these magical things for coincidence to be. Pi is one of these. We use pi…"

The conversation went on for some time, the boys

hanging on Opa's every word as he described these ideas as if they were a part of some giant mystery.

Passionately and deliberately, Opa explained complex concepts in ways the boys could easily understand. The boys soaked all of this in; Opa's examples hitting home with the boys in different ways.

As the discussion went on, Jimmy thought about what Opa said about the three of them being a team. Just because Mrs. Jackson has this crazy idea for math teams, didn't mean the three of them had to be a team for *everything*. Did it?

Still, Jimmy had forgotten over the past few years just how nice Jake was and never realized before how funny Lay could be. Even though they were both really smart, they never made Jimmy feel dumb. In fact, it was quite the opposite. Hanging around with these boys made Jimmy feel better about himself, and school.

Opa insisted on more than just the right answers. He pushed the boys to think about the problems in just a certain way. It was more about how to solve problems than simply coming up with the answers.

"It's how we apply ourselves that's the key," Jimmy remembered Opa saying. "Let me explain for a bit and you'll see. Yes, it's fine to memorize answers to some of these problems today, but what will you do tomorrow when there are twists in the fray? Yes, you must memorize the tools you'll need, like to multiply, divide and the value of pi; but when you know how to address the root of these problems, great things you'll achieve without much of a try."

It was true. Jimmy was now seen as one of the boys to look to for answers in math class. His grades were much improved, and he was actually having fun in class.

Jimmy smiled to himself for a moment, before the thought of his other friends came to mind. They gave him a pretty hard time about this whole thing. It wasn't really the part about getting better grades in math. It was the idea of hanging out with Jake and Lay. This just wasn't cool to his friends.

It made Jimmy feel a bit guilty. If it weren't for Jake picking him onto his team, Jimmy would just be suffering at the back of the class...as he always had.

On the other hand, Jimmy liked to win at sports and wouldn't be too likely to pick either Jake or Lay for dodgeball until no other boys were left. 'Was that so bad? Jake and Lay would understand,' he told himself.

Picking teams for kickball or dodgeball was completely different, wasn't it? Jimmy's lips pressed together, in that look he always got when he was thinking really hard about something.

"James, you look as if you are lost in thought," Opa said, springing Jimmy back to the discussion at hand. "Should I slow down, or repeat something I've taught?"

"No, no, sorry. Please go on," Jimmy shot back quickly. "Something else my mind was upon."

Jake and Lay laughed at that. The two boys had gotten so good at rhyming back to Opa, they hardly thought about it anymore. But Jimmy never rhymed back. Odd, Jimmy thought, that it happened without him even planning it. Jimmy laughed along with the rest of his team.

16

THE VISIT

"I'm not sure how much longer I'll be able to walk with you to school," Opa said one morning as he, Jake and Emily started on their morning route. "I'm afraid these old legs of mine stopped being a very useful tool."

Jake had noticed over the past few weeks, as the spring made signs of giving in to summer, that Opa's pace had slowed. He had taken to long naps during the day and often didn't eat dinner with the rest of the family. Still, his eyes remained clear and bright, as he pushed Jake and his team further every day.

"But, it makes me happy to walk with you on such a day," Opa continued with a smile, "with the spring flowers out – it's just too beautiful to say."

With that, Jake's mind wandered back to the previous summer. Opa so loved nature. One day while visiting Opa's cottage, hours and hours from the city, Jake found him lying out in the yard near the lake.

"Have you ever seen anything so beautiful?" Opa

whispered, staring straight up at the sky.

Jake nestled down beside him.

What a sight this must have been, as the two of them lie in the grass, their head inches from each other. Squinting away the sunlight and smiling like a child, Opa's face sparkled with pure joy.

The trees around the old cottage formed a canopy of dark brown and green. Set in a background of a deep blue sky, the huge tree limbs provided the much-needed shade from the hot Wisconsin summer.

"The trees, the sky – it's beautiful. It's just about as perfect as you could ever ask for," Opa breathed. "These are some pretty old Maples," pointing to the left a bit. "Soon I think they'll need to make way for some younger trees."

"They look fine to me, Opa." Jake said, sure nothing could take down these big old trees.

"They're huge - and strong, too. Look how big those branches are. They're like Elvis back home."

"Everything has its time, Jake, even Elvis." Opa said after a time. "At some point it is just *time* to move over and let the next generation in." Opa pointed to a stand of smaller trees growing in a rare sunny spot of the lawn.

"For maybe a thousand generations, for these trees, it has been so. The big tree must fall. And in its falling, it becomes the making of life for other trees and insects and animals too. Those smaller trees over there are probably the children of this big one here. At some point, it must give way to younger, stronger trees."

"Yes, Jake, it will fall and become the home for all kinds of life, big and small. Over the years, it will decay away into the soil, feeding all the rest of the trees left standing. It is the way of things, my little friend - all part of the plan." With that, Opa fell silent and just smiled at the sky.

"Mrs. Jackson wanted you to stop in and say hi," Jake said, his mind brought back to the present by the whistle of the crossing guard. Jake held Emmy's hand as they crossed the street. "Could you stop in before you say goodbye?"

"Absolutely, my lad, I most certainly could," Opa responded, still gazing at the spring flowers planted in the front yards they passed. "You've told me so much about her, I think I probably should."

The three of them made their way over to the Kindergarten wing of the school, making sure Emily got to her Pre-K class, before heading over to the main school building. On their way, they passed through the playground and ran into Jimmy Melder and his friends.

Jimmy didn't seem overly happy to see Opa here. He ignored Jake and his grandfather and walked right past them.

"What was that?" Jake said out loud, not really meaning to. It just made Jake mad that Jimmy walked right by Opa without even a *Good Morning* or anything.

Opa just chuckled.

"What's so funny, Opa?" Jake asked, made even more upset by his grandfather's seeming lack of understanding.

"I didn't have to pick him onto my team, and you didn't have to teach him all of that stuff. But I did... and you did - and he walks right by, pretending you're not even there. I should tell him I don't want him on my team anymore."

"You could do that of course, but do you think it would be right? To toss him out before you let him explain, and shed some light?"

Before Opa could say another word, Jake ran to catch up with Jimmy. "Hey, Jimmy! Opa is here, didn't you see."

Frankie, one of Jimmy's friends spun around and laughed. "Oh, Jimmy," he mocked, "your shrimpy little friend and his *great grandfather* are calling you! Jimmy, oh, Jimmy!"

This is just what Jimmy was trying to avoid. He wondered if Jake really understood the situation. 'I mean, doesn't he get it?' Jimmy thought. 'These are my friends and they don't hang out with the smaller kids like him.' Plus it just wasn't cool, in Jimmy's mind, to always have grown-ups around all the time.

Still, he started to feel guilty.

"Knock it off!" Jimmy said to his friends. At this point, he wasn't sure who he was more mad at; Jake, his friends, or himself. A million thoughts flooded Jimmy's mind. Memories of Opa's talks about courage and loyalty hit him like a brick.

The realization sunk in that Jake and Lay had never been anything but nice to him. This was more than he could say about his so-called '*friends*.'

They played kickball, dodgeball, and baseball together, but he'd begun to realize that the jabs they gave him about doing so well in math were really bugging him.

'What difference does it make to them?' he began to think. 'Were they bothered that I could actually do well in school? Were they threatened by it?'

"Jimmy, oh, Jimmy!" another jumped in.

Now Jimmy was really mad, but no longer at Jake. Jimmy was mad at himself and at these boys who he used to consider friends. He began to reach over to one of the boys, looking to grab his shirt.

"Oh, now that won't be necessary, will it?" a voice calmly said.

It was Opa. He'd caught up to the boys and was now looking on.

"No one gets hurt by simple banter such as this," he continued softly – putting his hand on Jimmy's shoulder. "You must decide to confront or dismiss."

"I was just about to confront it," Jimmy said in a frustrated voice.

"So I see," smiled Opa. "But maybe there is a better way. We needn't resort to blows; perhaps a challenge or game you can play?"

"What was that game you like so much," Opa

asked, now talking more loudly, "some game with a ball, where you dodge and such?"

"Dodgeball? Are you serious?" one of Jimmy's *friends* said. "We'd kill them!"

"Not if I were on their side," Jimmy said firmly.

"Get real, Jimmy!" the boy said. "You and the *brains* here have no chance against us."

"This is yet to be seen, my young friend," Opa smiled. "There is no telling what may happen in the end."

"Ha! Let's play at lunch," Jimmy's *friend,* Frankie, insisted.

"Can't today," Jake responded. "Remember, Mrs. Jackson has all the math teams in a special meeting at lunch today."

"All right, Mrs. Jackson is going to babysit the *brains* during lunch today so we'll have to take care of them next week," one of the boys said, as he pushed past Jimmy.

With that, Opa, Jake and Jimmy made their way into the school.

17

MRS. JACKSON'S SURPRISE

As usual, still well before the first bell of the day, there was no order in the hallway. A sea of kids seemed to move in every direction at once. Some walked, while others ran and dodged their way through the halls, ignoring the coaxings of the hall monitors.

Construction paper art, taped to the walls and lockers, flapped about as the doors opened and wind blew in. Jake, Jimmy and Opa navigated through the mess of boys and girls to Mrs. Jackson's classroom.

"Mrs. Jackson?" Jake asked, as he knocked on the open door.

"Yes, Jake?" Mrs. Jackson responded, as she looked up from the tests she'd been correcting.

"I'd like you to meet my grandfather, Mr. Clayton," Jake said.

"Good morning, Mrs. Jackson," Opa smiled. "It is a real pleasure to meet you. I've heard a great deal about you from Jake and his team."

Rising and moving around the desk, Mrs. Jackson

reached to shake Opa's hand. "The pleasure is mine, Mr. Clayton," she said firmly. Pointing to the young woman at the back of the classroom, "I'd like you to meet my assistant, Ms. Duffy."

Opa nodded.

"Boys, I'd like to chat with Jake's grandfather," Mrs. Jackson continued. "Would you give us a minute please?"

Jake and Jimmy headed off to their lockers. Jake's was down the hall a bit, Jimmy's was right outside of Mrs. Jackson's room, well within earshot.

Waiting until the boys had left the room, Mrs. Jackson gestured to the chair sitting beside her desk. "I haven't told the boys and girls this yet, but the school is going to host a Mathnastics tournament. We're going to talk about it today during lunch recess.

"I just wanted you to know how well Jake has been doing. I'm going to invite Jake and Lay Olson to be on one of the teams the fifth graders will enter. I'm going to put them on a team with Jill Dubois. Together they should do really well in the tournament."

Even over the ruckus in the hallway, Jimmy could hear the conversation. 'What should I expect?' he thought to himself, crushed. If he were to put together a dodgeball team, wouldn't he pick the very best players?

Still, the news cut him.

"What about James?" Opa asked, his eyes firmly fixed on Mrs. Jackson's.

"Oh, don't get me wrong, the work you've done with Jimmy has been nothing short of amazing. He is dyslexic, as you might know, and you have done wonders with him. But he is clearly the weak link on that team. I really think the team I'm suggesting could go very far in the tournament, perhaps beating some of the sixth or, even, seventh grade teams."

His head buried in his locker so no one could see his anguish, Jimmy's face showed the pain of the conversation happening just feet away.

Deflated, he felt, as if he got sucker-punched by one of the bigger kids on the playground. Tears started welling up in his eyes.

"Oh, I recognize you," Opa said after a pause. "You're a destination person." Mrs. Jackson looked very puzzled as Opa continued. "You see, I believe there are two types of people in this world, journey people and destination people. Journey people relish the challenges and the sights along the way. They seek communion with others who, likewise, can appreciate the joy and difficulty of the passage.

"Now destination people, on the other hand, would rather just be dropped off at the summit, avoiding the journey altogether. For them, you see, it is just being able to *say* they were there; never mind *how* they got there."

"I, sir, am not a destination person," Mrs. Jackson retorted, clearly unaccustomed to being challenged like this.

"All evidence to the contrary, Madam." Opa concluded quickly, his gaze still fixed on Mrs. Jackson's eyes. "These children have so much respect for you – as do I. And like me, you undoubtedly believe in excellence. You push these boys and girls for knowledge more than any other teacher. I see it every day. Take the next step – push them to accept responsibility. I don't have to point to the times in history where knowledge without responsibility has led to tragic results, do I? Now, no matter what, this won't end up in tragedy, but why miss an opportunity to teach the idea of making a choice and being responsible for the outcome?"

"If you want Jake to lead a team, push him to make the best decision. Tell him the options; the potentials of creating an *all-star* team. Now, I am not a big fan of all-star teams. They just aren't, well, teams. They tend to be a bunch of individuals who are out to show themselves in the best possible light."

"As far as James being dyslexic? My experience is that you can often substitute the word *brilliant* for *dyslexic*. You just have to help them frame things in ways that reveal their brilliance; allowing them to take advantage of the way their brains can run circles around everyone else's. James is like that...as was I. I am more than a bit surprised you do not see it in him."

"Now, were I a betting man, I would wager that Jake sees what I see." At that, Opa paused, smiled and stood in front of Mrs. Jackson's desk.

"I'm not sure what Jake will do, but I like the idea of giving him the opportunity to make the right decision. In any case, let Jake take responsibility for his actions. You are very good teacher, Mrs. Jackson. You are so close to being a *great* teacher. Don't miss out on an opportunity to take that next step."

With that, Opa politely nodded to both women in the room as if to say *Good Day* – and silently departed.

"Wow!" Ms. Duffy said in a half whisper.

"Tell me about it..." was Mrs. Jackson's only response.

18

CHOICES

Jimmy, having buried his head in his locker for the past few minutes, missed Opa's speech. Trying to get used to the idea that he *wasn't really* that good in math after all, Jimmy began to pull himself together. For the rest of the morning, Jimmy tried to maintain a positive face to the rest of the kids.

Still, he was surprised just how sad he'd become. Most of the boys and girls didn't notice, but Jake and Lay could see it, although they didn't say anything.

Lunchtime soon came. Jimmy cringed at the thought of the recess meeting Mrs. Jackson had arranged with the fifth grade's top four math teams.

"You may have heard," she started, "that we are hosting a district-wide Mathnastics meet. The fifth grade can send two teams to the meet.

"I originally called you here to tell you whom I've chosen to be on those teams. But, after giving it some thought, I decided a better option would be for the leaders of the top two teams to choose their members instead.

"Jake, your team finished first in the class. You get to choose two team members first. You can choose anyone in the class. If you want I can tell you who I think would do well in this competition, but you make the choice."

Before Mrs. Jackson could finish, Jake stood and said, "I already know who I want on my team."

"Would you like to hear some suggestions?" Mrs. Jackson questioned.

"No thank you," Jake said politely. "First, I choose Lay." This was obvious to everyone, nods all around the classroom.

"You can pick anyone, Jake. There are some very bright boys and girls in this class," said Mrs. Jackson.

"I'm going to pick someone very bright," Jake said, smiling.

At this point, Jimmy had sunk into his chair waiting to hear the name Jill, Madison, or even Justin.

"Jimmy," Jake said, and sat down.

Jimmy, shocked but elated, sat tall in his seat once more. After overhearing the conversation between Opa and Mrs. Jackson earlier, Jimmy thought a lot about this. If asked to pick a team to win at dodgeball, would he pick Jake or Lay? Probably not. But now he began to feel much differently about things. He remembered back to a story Opa told.

"Loyalty," Opa started, "is not about convenience or about being there only when things are good. It is all about being there when things get difficult and staying when no others would. Loyalty, you see, is about making a simple decision everyday; do you choose to ignore, to go - or do you stay?"

Jimmy began to understand the message. You

make a decision to be loyal. Loyalty is a choice you make every day.

Jimmy smiled and the rest of the class didn't seem too surprised. Jimmy had become quite respected by the other teams. Jake's math team stayed together - for a few more weeks anyway. Four Fridays from now was the day of the big tournament.

Usually a month seemed so far away, but Jimmy immediately felt very nervous. He wondered if he'd be up to the task, and worried about letting his teammates down. 'Imagine that,' he thought.

Mark Fralick

19

PAST AND FUTURE

Excited, Jake ran all the way home that Friday, proud to tell Opa all about his team going to the Mathnastics tournament next month. Up the sidewalk he ran and up to the door, just in time to help his mom and Emily bring in some groceries. Together they opened the door to their house.

To everyone's amazement, there - parked in the middle of their living room - stood a very, very large telescope. Peering into the eyepiece like a deep space explorer, stood Opa.

"Daddy," Jake's mom started, "what's this?"

"This, my dear," Opa said, not looking up from the eyepiece, "is a telescope."

What an understatement! This was no dime-store toy. Over eight feet long, the telescope had an aiming lens and a tripod that made it taller than anyone or anything in the room. Opa had it aimed into the heavens through the large picture window in the front of the house. This device was immense.

"Wow!" Jake smiled in amazement. No one

seemed to be able to move in their surprise. After a long pause, Jake's mom just shook her head and took the groceries into the kitchen. Opa simply continued to adjust the aiming knobs and smiled.

After dinner, Opa took Jake on his *Guided Tour of the Solar System*. The Moon, Mars and Jupiter all shined brightly that night. "Looking through a telescope gives us a direct view of history; we can see things that to the naked eye would long stay a mystery."

Jake looked puzzled.

"Jake," Opa continued, "what do we see when we look through this telescope?"

"Stuff – like planets and moons," Jake responded.

"Stuff? Stuff indeed!" Opa snorted. "We see light and we see the past. You see, one of the constants in this universe of ours is the speed of light. Here on Earth, because it is so fast - light speed seems pretty, well, instant. But the reality is that it moves at a set pace. Since most of these stars are far, far away – it can take years and years for the light to get here.

"So, when we are looking out into space, we are seeing what happened in the past. Some of those stars whose light will just now show; may not now exist – having sent its light on its way millions of years ago. For me, my lad, this is a very special treat. It is the point at which the past and the present come together and meet. Look at this star right there," he continued, as he aimed the telescope for Jake.

"What you are looking at is how this star appeared when you were just born. Yes, what a day that was – you were born just as the night became morn. A beautiful day, no clouds could be found; so happy I was – I couldn't utter a sound.

"And this star here," repositioning the telescope again, "as it now appears; is as it was when I was a lad of just 2 years. And this one," swinging the telescope around again, "is like no other; this is the year I married your grandmother." At that, Opa paused a moment – deep in thought.

"Let's go further back," Jake said, peering intently into the eyepiece of the telescope. "Let's go further back – show me more; what stars were like years and years before."

"Hmm," Opa mumbled, as he looked into an old book he used to navigate the telescope. "Ah, now here's one that is especially keen; maybe the farthest star yet to be seen. Long, long ago the light from this star's journey started; long before Lincoln, the Pilgrims, or even Columbus departed.

"Big is the space outside of our protected little sphere; even our closest neighbors are not very near.

But it reminds me often, as I look up at a star; what a wonderful place is this, and how lucky we are. For in all the galaxies and all those planets and stars; we are so very lucky to share our lives with a family such as ours."

The telescope, Jake learned, became a way of showing the boys how to focus on details. Later that evening, Opa had the boys do an exercise.

"A telescope magnifies, but it also pulls your eye to one spot. In all the great heavens that you can see, it allows you to focus on just one thing – whatever you are aiming at. When we are working on problems, sometimes it is hard for us to focus like that. We have no magnifying glass or telescope to narrow our view; we must create our own focus - right out of the blue."

"Pick a plane from across the room," Opa continued, "and tell me about it."

Jake was quick to answer the question. "I see a *P-51 Mustang*. It is mostly silver, as many of them were, and it has the *Army Air Corps* logo on the wings."

"Okay, very good Jake," Opa said, looking closely at the *P-51*. "But you are not focusing on details. Boys, let's look at that *Mustang*. Let's focus only on the wing – tell me what you can see."

"I see the curved shape of the wing," started Jimmy, "and there is a spot at the front of the wing that has a gun or something sticking out of it."

"Yes," Lay began, "and a couple of warning stickers on the wing. One says *No Step* and the other I can't read. There is a black strip of something where the wing connects to the rest of the plane."

Together Opa and the boys looked at that plane at

a level of detail that the boys found exhausting. "Can we stop now?" Jake pleaded, "I'm getting really tired."

"Yes," Opa replied quickly. While done more for the benefit of Jimmy, this exercise helped the entire group become calm and focused. "But hold your thinking at this level of detail and listen to this word problem."

Opa read a word problem that had a number of details plainly stated but also several that were assumed.

The boys quickly identified all the details that were stated. "Ah, there is more here," Opa encouraged. "It is simple, sometimes, to identify the details easily stated; but hidden facts or cloudy ideas may need to be debated. Look more closely, keep a keen view. Focus on finding any stray clue."

For hours the boys pulled apart problems, leaving no stone unturned; sorting the required information from the text. Jimmy found he had a real knack for visualizing the problems. This was not lost on the other two boys.

Mark Fralick

20

MIND'S EYE

The next afternoon Opa talked to Jake, Jimmy and Lay about the upcoming competition. "It will be so cool - I can't wait," Jake said excitedly. "We are going to beat *everyone* and I'll actually be able to say I was the *best*."

"Oh, really," Opa said to this, before Jake could continue. Jake knew this question. It was a question with a point. It wasn't Opa being surprised. This was Opa asking Jake to reconsider his statement. Jake paused.

"Isn't it okay to be proud of what we are able to do?" Jake questioned.

"We worked hard," Jimmy added, "and we can finally beat all of those kids who are usually teasing us about not being as smart as them. We can go back to them and say *oh, you weren't as good as us – too bad*."

"Is this why you do this?" Opa asked, sounding very disappointed. "Boys, many kinds of bullies in this world you'll find; some bullies of strength, some bullies of mind. Far worse are those who belittle for their gain. Much more damage can be done with words without restrain. Is this why you do this?"

"No, Opa."

"Why then?"

"Well," Jake started slowly, "I think it's really cool to be part of something like this. I mean, we have a lot of fun and we are learning a lot. I'm having more fun in school than I ever had before."

With that, Jake shot his grandfather, a look as if to say *'how's that?'*

Jake's grandfather smiled. "I am very happy for you and your friends, but not because you may fare well in some competition. For me it is all about the journey and this team becoming friends."

After a short pause Opa continued, *'I believe it is indeed a good year; if it's a year that you make one good friend to draw near. People come and go from our lives all the time you see; but a friend, a true friend, now that is a rare gift to me. You boys will have the best gift of all – very good friends you three will be."*

"I think," Opa continued, "that too often it is the bad and sad memories we take with us on our trip to becoming grown. I will tell you a little secret, it needn't be so. But, it takes some effort.

"When you are happy, or if there is something that you really want to remember when you grow older, you must take a snapshot in your mind and burn it into your memory. Let's all do it now, shall we? There will be days when you feel horribly bad – maybe something tragic has happened. There will absolutely be days like that; the mathematics of life demands it."

"Unfortunately, sooner than you know it, you will have a horribly bad day. But, that is not *this* day. Today is a great day. Look around at each other, think about all that you've done together and burn the feeling and the image into your mind. Now close your eyes, and really *see* it in your mind's eye. Take a big breath; smell the spring flowers, the lilacs."

As one, the four of them breathed deep the scene around them, and together, the three boys opened their eyes. For some reason, Opa kept his eyes closed for an extra moment. When they finally opened, he witnessed the looks on the young faces around him. It became obvious to Opa that it was his face, at this moment, which the boys were burning into their memory. Opa smiled at this thought.

All of this drove Jimmy deep into thought. Were these his *real* friends? The boys he usually hung out with hadn't been very nice to him lately. Shouldn't they be happy that he'd been doing so well in school? They would be happy for him - if they were *really* his friends.

Opa saw the questions in Jimmy's eyes. "Jimmy, look at me," Opa said, softly.

"People rotate in and out of our lives like constellations. But this strange attractor called friendship becomes a kind of gravity that pulls some of us together. And so we share this orbit called life with each other, for a time anyway.

"You see, friends always support your journey to become the best version of *you*. They will never ask you to be a lesser or different version because of jealousy, envy or their own self-centered desires.

"Now, there is a simple test to see who your

friends really are. Friends never miss an opportunity to be there for each other. Lads, there will be great times when you are there for each other in celebration. There will also be days where you will feel each other's pain. This separates friends from the people just *spinning* around you. Without calling, without asking, and without fail, friends are always there for each other."

Now looking at all the boys with those sharp eyes of his, Opa said in a firm voice, "Never miss an opportunity to be there for your friends. Do you understand?"

As one, came the response, "Yes, sir."

Jimmy realized that this is exactly what has been going on. At every step of this journey, his new friends, Opa, Jake, and Lay had been there for him. Whether it was simply picking him for the team or giving him a way to surprise Mrs. Jackson, they had been there for him all the way.

Shocked at what he was feeling, Jimmy couldn't speak. He realized that this was one of those times Opa talked about - a time that he always would want to remember. He looked at his friends, all close around him, closed his eyes and etched the image, and this feeling, forever into his mind.

Opening his eyes, Jimmy realized the discussion had moved back to math. Opa's eyes had a glint of wonder as he spoke. "Remember we talked about how to calculate slope? Well, what happens if the slope of a surface, like a real road, is constantly changing? We are going to talk now about something really fun, I'm sure it will be something your classmates have never done..."

21

LULLABIES AND LISTENING

Later that evening, since Jake's mom was working late, Opa got Jake and Emily ready for bed.

"Do we want a story tonight?" he asked, walking into their darkened room.

Every night it was the same question, followed by the same answer.

"Yes, please," Emily said with anticipation.

Nighttime stories for Opa were not the typical type. They weren't old fables or fairytales. Opa made them up to suit what Emily wanted to hear about. Actually, Opa had done this for Jake too, when he was younger – asking him what he wanted a story about each night.

Jake had become quite a good storyteller, taking over for Opa or Mom sometimes when Emily wanted a story. Emily usually wanted a story about something that happened to her that day. Or, she'd want a story about one of her favorite cartoon characters doing something funny. Tonight she wanted a story that Opa had told her and Jake many times.

"*Snowfake tory!* Yeah, tell that one," she said, as she eased her head into her feather-filled pillow. Every night it was the same. "Yeah, tell that one," she'd say.

Jake liked this one too, so he listened in.

Opa started in a soft voice;

"There once was a little snowflake crisp and clean,
A wonderful snowflake unlike any other you've seen;
It was born from the clouds and in the wind it blew,
On a cold winter day, peacefully it flew;

Fun she was having, flitting about and floating,
Beautiful she was, even if she was gloating;
But wait, she said — what is that I see,
The ground, it's the ground that's ahead of me;

Shhh came a voice - don't be afraid,
We're all joining together in a snow bank be laid;

Opa's Rhyme

But I like floating around myself she said in a tone,
Don't worry said the other — you'll like not being alone;
Will it hurt? the little snowflake asked — feeling very unsure,
No, you'll be something more, not just a snowflake demure;

And that's just what happened — and happily she smiled,
For her friends everywhere - and all around her were piled;
They were piled high, you see, she and her friends were stacked,
Closely they mingled - tightly they packed;

A beautiful snow bank they were as the days came and went,
But spring soon came and this seemed not all heaven sent;
You see the warm afternoons started the snow bank to melt,
The snowflake was afraid again — uncertain she felt;

Shhh came a calm voice from far behind her once more,
You don't remember this from time and time before?
The little snow flake frowned as she thought and thought,
Trying hard to remember - but coming up with naught;
This is what we do you see - with a smile the other said,
We'll melt into this river and to a big lake we'll be led;

For a time in rivers and lakes we'll happily stay,
With all of our friends we'll swim and together we'll play;
Then some of us will become fog, hanging heavy and low,
Or clouds light and dark - clouds fast and slow;
You'll like it, you'll like it — please, please trust in me,
Believe what I say, just you wait and see;

So into the river that ran far and wide, she was sent,
The river churned with her friends and faster it went;
Until at last into a great lake were they finally plunked,
A blue and windswept lake — in waves they were dunked;
The long summer they spent together, all her friends, as one,
Until they began to evaporate beneath the hot sun;

I don't want to leave my friends – I just know they'll cry,
Don't worry said the other, we're all headed to the sky;
Again in the clouds they floated, for many days and nights,
But soon winter came with her cruel wind that bites;
And into a snowflake once more she happily turned,
Not scared this time from all she had learned;

On the wind she blew and ahead she now heard,
Soft and muffled sobbing another snowflake purred;
Shhh she said to the other snowflake - Please don't be afraid,
We're all joining together and in a snow bank we'll be laid;
Time and time before – you have done this too,
It's just part of life's circle - it's just what we do."

Opa sat silently for a long moment. Emily, now fast asleep, didn't hear much of the story. Jake felt as if the story was being told to him, although Opa kept gently stroking Emily's back. Jake hadn't heard this story for some time.

"I tell Em one like that," Jake said, softly. "Well, it isn't exactly that - but kinda like it. It's called the wave story."

"I'd like to hear it some time," Opa said, as he leaned over to Jake. "Perhaps one day soon I shall ask you to tell it to me."

"Opa," Jake said, in a very soft whisper, "I don't want things to change. I like things just like they are right now. I know life is a big circle. I remember you telling me about the trees at the cottage - and the snowflake is kind of like that too. Can't it just stay like this for a while?"

"Hmm," came a whispered chuckle from Opa. "I

wish that too, my young lad. But it is not the way of things – though it needn't be sad. Each ending is a new beginning in my book, no matter how sad a single moment might look."

"Sometimes," Jake began softly, "at night I hear you saying some type of rhyme or something before the day's end. Is it a prayer you are doing or a new story - to me you can lend?"

"Yes Jake," Opa said, surprised by the question. "A prayer of sorts..."

"Do you believe in God?" Jake asked solemnly.

After a long pause, Opa said "Believe? God? Yes, I believe there is a God. Not a God of favors, miracles or magic; instead, a God who has empowered us with a gift of incredible power - the power to choose our own way.

"Yes, I believe in God. You see, there is a force in this universe called Entropy. It is a steady march toward chaos – an ever-present push toward decline and disorder. Yet, we evolve. The gift of life is a direct contradiction of this force pushing everything to disintegration. I know there are religions that abhor the idea of evolution.

"Funny I think it is that some religions feel so compelled to fight knowledge. When knowledge is your enemy, then ignorance is your ally. In the history of man, no good has ever come when men seek council with ignorance.

"No, I believe knowledge can bring us closer to God, and I think evolution *is* God's plan. I feel we have a mission while we are still here; a charter. We must further evolve as beings, as students of life – to realize the value of the gift with which we've been blessed.

"We are the stewards of Humanity. We must pay it forward and help the next generation to further evolve. Without God, my young friend, we decline; we dissolve into chaos and disaster. You see, my lad, God expresses himself through us.

"God has given us the ability to make decisions, choose right from wrong, to choose to be kind and to love. Or to hate, be cruel, horrible and become the worst version of ourselves.

"The history of man is riddled with the best and worst examples of humanity. We must choose where we stand. Once, a great and wonderful man, a gift to the people of earth, said that the *Kingdom of God is within each of us.*

"Now, if we believe that God can be within each of us, we must also accept the opposite; that it is possible to be swayed by hatred, sadness, and jealously. This is called evil. This too, this dark way, is within us.

"Here is how it can happen, my young friend. Sadness can become despair; despair becomes hate. Hatred leads to evil.

"You see, some people have this view of evil being *'out there'* somewhere, like this evil figure is somehow walking the earth.

"You can understand it, can't you? This idea removes some of the responsibility we all have every day to fight evil within ourselves and to do the right thing.

"But no, my lad, both good and evil exists within each of us. We need to understand this and confront it. We must choose to be strong, choose to do what is right – every day. But that doesn't mean we don't need help sometimes."

After a long pause, Opa continued, "Jake, you are blessed with time on your side. The future is your friend. For me, I am afraid, time is no longer my ally, the future no longer bright.

"Sometimes I need help remembering that I have been blessed with the gift of insight and I have the ability to deal with this and not despair. So, I pray. I pray because it makes me a better listener.

"I know people often pray for things, for events, for help. I would never be so arrogant as to actually *ask* for something from God. For me, that is not what praying is about; and I don't think this is how the universe works anyway.

"Praying, for me, is seeking to reveal the power of God that is already inside of us. I pray to be reminded of what I already know – that there is great power in each of us.

"So, each night I say this short prayer, a version of an old prayer I heard long, long ago."

"Dear Lord,
Grant that I may seek to comfort rather than to be comforted,
To understand than to be understood,
To love than to be loved,
It is by forgiving that one is forgiven,
For it is in giving that we receive,
and it is by dying that we awake to Eternal Life.
Amen"

"Yes, Jake, I pray because it makes me a better listener."

Mark Fralick

22

THE MATH OF LIFE

With only two days left to Mathnastics, the boys spent the evening in Jake's room, working through problems. Most of these evenings passed with Opa happily watching on - coaching and challenging the boys. The boys had indeed come a long way.

Opa smiled and sat quietly near the door. They could handle almost any problem he threw at them. But, for Opa, this wasn't the real success.

The true success was seeing Jake happy again and knowing he had friends who, Opa knew, would be there for him. This, more than anything, is what made Opa so happy.

For a long time Opa had thought about the meaning of this time in his life. He wondered how he would handle it. As his body failed him, would he lash out, crawl into a shell, or wallow in self-pity?

Opa always knew the math. At some point the math of life dictates some very bad days in each of our lives. But, the choice of how to face them, that was ours to determine.

It turns out that these boys had saved him in a way. He'd been able to spend time with Jake yet still make sure he would be okay - with good, trusted friends.

'That's it,' Opa thought to himself – dying is the easy part; living after your loved ones pass on - that is the hard part. Dying, no matter what happens afterward, just happens and it is done. But Jake would live on for scores and scores of years. It was important to Opa that Jake be prepared for the mountain of time ahead of him.

"Opa, could you explain standard deviation again?" Jake asked. "It probably won't be on any of the skill sheets on Friday, but it doesn't hurt to be prepared for it."

"Right you are," Opa said, springing from his thoughts. "Certainty, my lads. Standard deviation helps us understand certainty. It can help us understand volatility of results…" Opa and the boys talked about math and life until bedtime.

23

CAUSE AND EFFECT

'A big day,' Jake thought to himself about the Mathnastics meet tomorrow. Still, he had to get through *this* day. The school day had not started well. The school bullies never missed an opportunity to pick on the boys, which now included Jimmy.

It was lunchtime and the three had just taken their normal spots at one of the tables with their packed lunches and pads of paper and pencils to practice problems.

Frankie, one of Jimmy's old bully *friends*, decided he needed to sit next to Lay. Two others flanked Jake on the other side of the table.

"What's going on guys?" Jimmy asked, already knowing what was going to happen next.

"Well," started Frankie, "we were wondering what these boys were eating that keeps them so puny."

"Knock it off Frankie," Jimmy said forcefully.

"Why? Whose gonna make me?" Somehow Jimmy knew that was coming.

"Look," said Lay, "what is the deal? We're better

at math, you're better at dodgeball. Can't you guys just do your thing and let us do ours?"

"What's that?" mocked Frankie. "Did I just hear some squeaking from the pipsqueak?"

Jimmy's face was turning beet red. Jake looked over and could see him heading for a blow-up.

"I don't think they're that much better than us at dodgeball!" Jake blurted out defiantly.

"What?" laughed the bully, "you have got to be kidding. We'd kill you!"

"Really?" said Lay, in a matter-of-fact sort of voice, taking a casual bite from his sandwich. "And you know this because ....?"

"Because you guys are runts who probably can't even throw the ball," Frankie said, almost yelling now. "That's how!"

"Hmmm," Lay smiled, with his head cocked at a slight angle and his eyes feigning surprise. For whatever reason, Jake and his friends no longer feared these boys. They just weren't in the mood to be pushed around anymore.

While this conversion was going on, and unnoticed by the bullies, Lay had been fumbling with a straw. "Do you remember the idea of cause and effect we talked about in science?" Lay asked of Frankie, who was now leaning into his *personal space* - trying to intimidate him.

There was no answer from Frankie, just more not-so-subtle leaning and pushing from him.

"See, for every action," Lay continued, as he raised his hand about a foot above the table, "there is an equal and opposite reaction!" With that, he smashed his hand into his Twinkie on the table.

He'd spent the past couple minutes inserting a short straw through the wrapper of his Twinkie and into its creamy center. The straw, now pointed directly at Frankie's face, shot a ferocious stream of Twinkie filling right up his nose.

Frankie immediately recoiled and coughed violently. The kids at the table exploded in laughter.

A stunned Frankie fumed. It wasn't just the fact that he'd been assaulted with a creamy dessert cake that got him so steamed. It was the idea that this shrimp would even *think* he could get away with something like this. Just as he was about to take a swing at Lay, Jake caught his arm.

"You guys wanted a match a couple weeks ago, how about during playground time in five minutes?" Jake blurted out, trying to deflect some of the anger.

The team correctly understood that sometimes you cannot avoid your foes; and when you cannot avoid them, you need to deal with them head-on. Well, there was no avoiding them now.

'What would the harm be in confronting them?' Jake surmised. Even if they lost the match, which was likely, they may gain the respect of the bullies. Jake knew that bullies were not apt to pick on difficult prey.

"Most bullies, you see," Opa had once said, "are lazy – they seek only easy targets. If you want to avoid bullies and, later in life, thugs and robbers, don't be an easy target!"

The bullies left the table. Frankie, cleaning up his face, exited the lunchroom hastily, itching to dismantle the boys at dodgeball. Even more than that, Frankie hoped to inflict some *real* punishment this time.

Mark Fralick

24

SPECTACULAR PLANS

"Well, that went well!" Lay said with a smirk. He had a knack for making funny, if slightly *off*, comments. He was the quiet, wisecracker of the group. Jake and Jimmy always laughed with Lay, even if the other kids didn't quite *get* him. Together, the boys laughed as they recounted the events of the past few minutes.

"Okay," started Jake. "so I thought a dodgeball duel might just get them off our backs."

"Maybe," admitted Jimmy, adding, with a smirk, "if you guys survive!"

Together, the three mapped out a survival strategy that Jimmy had obviously been thinking about for some time. It was a high-risk, high-reward plan, which would lead to great success or spectacular failure.

Opa often spoke of his admiration for those unafraid of huge public failures.

"I applaud spectacular failures!" he would often say. "Without those failures, or the *risk* of them," he insisted, "there would never be amazing successes. Only those confident enough to endure the potential of a spectacular failure would become a great success."

Either way, in this case, it would likely end their bully problems for good.

25

SHOWDOWN

Word spread on the playground; a dodgeball battle between the bullies and the brains at noon. They'd use playground rules, what the kids called *Killer* rules.

In this version of dodgeball you can only be *killed*, you can't be added back if someone else on your team catches a ball. Once you're done, you're done. Usually it made for quick games, fitting the twenty-two minute playground break they got after lunch.

Mostly blacktop, the playground area butted up against the sidewall of the school. There, between a couple of smaller walls that jutted out from the sidewall, was the perfect spot for a makeshift dodgeball court.

The sun of this spring day had warmed the blacktop. With the lunchtime temperature pushing well passed 60, jackets would not be needed. Unfortunately, this put the advantage in the bullies' hands, as this meant it would be easier to throw the balls really hard.

Some of the onlookers put their jackets and

sweatshirts down to mark the outside corners and out-of-bounds line. The stage was set.

Jake, Lay and Jimmy approached the court; Jimmy quietly giving last second instructions. The bullies, already on the court, angrily heaved red playground balls against the school's brick wall.

The boys shed their jackets and headed to the center court. The bullies laid three mid-sized balls and one small *killer* ball on the center line.

The *killer* ball was a smaller red playground ball, small enough so that most kids could easily grip it firmly with one hand and hurl it with great velocity. It was a particularly punishing projectile.

As Jake approached the center line he announced, "Normal Killer rules, three on each side, one ball start, last one in - wins." One ball start means that when you run from the back line to the front to start the game, you can only pick up one ball. Jake turned and headed to the back line.

"Head shots are good," he heard, as he approached the back line. No, it was not one of the bullies, but Lay who made this provocative statement. The bullies looked at each other, a bit perplexed. The boys and girls looked around for teachers in the area.

Head shots in dodgeball were strictly off limits at recess. If caught by a teacher, the purposeful toss at someone's noggin would surely earn you study hall for the next few days.

The little crowd of boys and girls stirred at this development. This was part of the strategy Jimmy came up with. It was pretty unlikely that one of the bullies would take a head shot during recess. But the move showed everyone that Lay, the smallest of the bunch, was simply unafraid.

The bullies set themselves on the back line, as did Jimmy's team. Everyone was set. Jimmy looked at his team and nodded. "One, two, three, go!" he shouted.

All three bullies lunged to the center court, each going for a ball. On Jimmy's side, only he ran up to the center line.

Getting there first, he grabbed the small ball and, at the same time, started another ball rolling toward the back of the court, toward his waiting teammates.

"Foul, foul," insisted one of the bullies. Rolling a ball backwards at the start of the game was not against the rules, but it was not ever done before either.

"I only picked up one ball!" Jimmy responded. All the boys moved to the middle of their sides of the court. By this time, Jake had picked up the other ball; each side had two.

Lay stood between Jimmy and Jake. Small but quick, Lay was a great dodger but didn't throw well. One of the bullies eyed Lay up for a leg shot. He hurled the ball. Just as he did so, Jimmy took a shot at him.

Both balls missed their marks; Lay aptly dodged the leg shot and Jimmy's toss was far off the mark.

The other bully with a ball saw an opportunity; Lay and Jimmy were unarmed. He set up a shot. At this point, Jake tossed his ball over to Jimmy. The bully now had a clear shot at the much slower Jake. He took the shot.

Unknown to the bullies was the fact that while Jake was slow, he was a great catch. He had an odd, but effective, technique when catching low throws. Jake would allow the ball to bounce off his arms straight into the air. Then, with much of the speed now taken off the ball, it would float down for an easy catch. Jake called this the *Super Scooper*.

The bully's toss was a bit higher than the foot-shot he tried for. This allowed Jake to use his *Super Scooper* move to perfection. The ball bounced off his angled and out-stretched arms as it bounded up above his head. It came down in his arms in an easy catch.

'One down, two to go,' Jake thought. The crowd of boys and girls cheered as one of the bullies exited the court. Jimmy took another shot. This time, Jimmy's shot ran straight and true and took out the bully at his shin. The boys and girls cheered.

The cheers were short-lived though. By this time, the other bully had fetched the first ball Jimmy tossed over and heaved it at Jimmy's legs.

A hit! Almost planting his face into the blacktop with the force of the impact, Jimmy was out with a wicked foot shot. The boys and girls were suddenly silenced.

It did not look good for Jake and Lay. Yes, they had three balls on their side, but the last boy left, Howie, was the biggest of the bullies, and threw harder than anyone else in school.

Howie was huge, with very pale skin and dark hair. Jake thought this boy looked a bit like Frankenstein. Just put a couple of bolts into his neck and Howie would be *Frankenboy*! But *Frankenboy* had a wicked throw, there could be no doubt.

Howie grinned widely. Lay, now holding a ball, stood next to Jake. The small *killer* ball was behind him by a step or two just in case one of them needed it. They seemed frozen, as if not sure what to do next.

Howie knew! Howie hurled his ball directly at Lay's kneecaps. There was no way Lay had time to get out of the way. His reaction was to lower his hands and try to deflect the on-coming projectile with the ball he was holding.

The ball collided violently with Lay's, almost dislodging his grip, and bounced harmlessly toward the back of their court. Even though all four balls were on their side of the court, this match was far from over. Howie was a very difficult *out*.

Jake and Lay each moved to the center of the court with two balls. Jake with two regular sized playground balls, Lay with one of these and the small *killer* ball. They needed to get close to the center line, as neither of them was a strong thrower.

They looked at each other and, almost in unison, tossed their balls at Howie. It was a close miss on both counts.

In a stunning move, Jake turned his back to Howie and ran to the back of the court. Howie could not resist this. He grabbed one of the balls off a bounce and quickly hurled it at Jake's back.

"Out!" he yelled as it hit Jake solidly between the shoulders. With a quick fist in the air to celebrate, Howie looked around for the other ball that had been thrown at him.

In that instant, something odd happened to Howie. As he turned, Lay delivered a perfect head shot with the *killer* ball.

Howie had come too near to the center line, and while focused on an imaginary target on Jack's back, had neglected to see Lay off to the side, just a few feet away. Lay did not hesitate after Howie released his ball on Jake. Lay's ball struck him firmly on the side of the face.

The playground erupted with shouts and screams for Jimmy's team. For a moment Frankie yelled "Head shot, doesn't count," before remembering that Lay included these at the beginning of the game. The three bullies seemed to disappear in the mob of boys and girls celebrating the victory.

As Jimmy exchanged high-fives with his team, the bell rang, ending recess. They got in the line for Mrs. Jackson's homeroom and filed into school.

While putting his sweatshirt back into his locker, Jake felt a forceful tug on his shirt. Frankie spun Jake around, pinning him to his locker. "You think you won? You didn't win anything!" Frankie spat in anger; his fist clenched and rearing back.

"Knock it off, Frankie!" came a voice from behind him. It was Howie. "They beat us. It was a good game. Get over it." Howie grabbed Frankie's arm and, in an odd turn, pinned Frankie against the lockers. "Don't be such a sore loser!"

He gave Frankie a bit of a nudge as if to say *I don't want to have to say this again* – and gave Jake a smile. "Good game," he said, as he released Frankie and made his way to his locker.

Frankie, now seeming just small and sad to Jake, turned and disappeared into the crowd of boys and girls heading back to class.

Mark Fralick

26

AFTER FURTHER REVIEW

That night the team replayed the events of the day to Opa, who enjoyed the telling of the tale. "It was Jimmy's idea to use Jake as a decoy," Lay said.

"Once I got the small ball, I knew I would have the last shot. Those bigger balls are kind of big for me, but that killer ball is perfect. I can really get a good grip on it. I just focused on Howie's big old head, and tossed right at it. Knocked him flat and that was that!"

"A good plan indeed," Opa commented. "You put your smallest teammate in the position to make the biggest play, and he came through for you. It's not unlike Bart Starr's run for the Green Bay Packers in the *Ice Bowl*, a long time ago."

"They gave the ball to Starr, one of the smallest guys on the team. All the bigger men cleared a narrow gap for Starr, allowing him to score. So, you proved that acting together and as a team; everyone plays a part, no matter how small their stature may seem. This, you see, is the difference between a team and a throng; and tomorrow doing the same, working as a team, you can do no wrong. If you do this, my young friends, even if you do not win the day; victorious, in my book, you will be, no matter what the scores say."

"Okay, let's review some strategies," Opa continued, after a short pause. Together, Opa and the boys exchanged ideas on how to handle the different sorts of problems they imagined would be thrown at them tomorrow.

Jimmy, with his great imagination and keen visualization abilities, set the strategies.

Lay, with his near perfect math skills, would execute the strategies.

Jake, gifted with an incredible knack for detail, did the quality control and reviewed the work.

Excited about the prospects of the coming day, the boys focused on preparation.

27

MATHNASTICS

A lot more kids than I thought, Lay observed to himself. That was an understatement.

Fifth through eighth graders flooded their school cafeteria, each group chaperoned by a teacher. Lay was surprised that so many kids made it here only thirty minutes after the end of the normal school day.

Mrs. Jackson's two groups were sitting at the designated fifth grade table.

"Now, what is going to happen," she began, "is that we will be split into sections. Usually, a section is the same as your grade level, but you can choose to challenge another grade by signing up into their section. So Jake, you may want to try the sixth grade section if you want to challenge them."

Jake, Jimmy and Lay smiled at that statement. "Finally," Mrs. Jackson continued, "there is an open-class section that is for the advanced middle school classes, but you don't need to worry about that. When they move you to the competition sections, make sure you are in the grade in which you want to compete."

Within a few minutes, all the kids in the cafeteria started to file out into the section areas. Jake led his team through the doors, out of the cafeteria.

Hours passed as late afternoon gave into evening. Looking exhausted, the boys and girls of the Mathnastics competition finally began trickling back into the cafeteria. Lay, Jimmy and Jake made their way back to their home table. Mrs. Jackson eagerly awaited a report.

"Well, I don't know how we did, but it was fun!" Lay said. The boys laughed; tired, but pleased by their efforts.

"Great," Mrs. Jackson said, smiling. "In 20 or 30 minutes they will announce winners of the sections and which *open-class* teams get invited back for the city-wide Power Round tomorrow morning.

"You have time to grab something to eat if you want," she said, as she stood and began chatting with one of the other teachers.

The boys, along with Madison and her group got in line for a snack. Lay and Madison compared notes about the difficulty of the math.

Soon, teachers started to collect near the award table pulled to the front of this large, echoing room. A microphone stand stood next to a table filled with trophies.

"I would like to congratulate all the students for an excellent competition. We are going to announce sections winners starting with the fifth grade section," one of the teachers said. The room quieted.

"In third place is the Packer Backer team from the Cabrini Middle School," she said. The room responded with enthusiastic applause as the Cabrini team accepted their trophies.

"In second place, we have Montgomery Middle School - the Math Bears." After the ribbons for second place were proudly collected, the teacher continued.

"In first place for the fifth grade section..." At this, Mrs. Jackson's teams looked at each other with excited anticipation. "The Math Nuts from Silverbrook Intermediate School!"

The boys leapt to their feet and cheered loudly. Madison's cheeks turned red, almost matching her fiery locks. She was smart, but shy, not accustomed to attention. Her team screamed with happiness as it sunk in.

They'd won! Madison's *Math Nuts* team brought home the first place trophy to Silverbrook's fifth grade. Madison's team, along with Mrs. Jackson, stood for pictures as Jimmy, Lay and Jake applauded loudly.

As the fifth grade victors returned to the table, Jake's team stood and met them with high-fives. "Now, let's see how you guys did," Madison said, knowing Jake's *Sea Bees* team didn't compete in the fifth grade section.

Soon, the sixth grade section awards were announced. Mrs. Jackson's teams waited as patiently as possible as the teacher read the winning teams.

"First place in the sixth grade section goes to... the Badgers, from Badger Middle School."

The boys stood and applauded politely and quietly sat back at the table. Mrs. Jackson glanced at Jake - who gave a sort of *its okay* shrug back to her.

The boys were happy with their efforts after all - no matter what the result. Jake's team and Maddie's team chatted quietly while the other trophies were announced.

"Finally," the teacher at the microphone said, with more than a bit of excitement, "we have the three open-class teams that will represent our school district in the *Power Round*, held right here tomorrow morning. These teams have truly shown that they have earned a place in the city-wide competition."

The teacher paused, letting the gravity of the moment sink in.

"In third place we have the eighth grade team from Marquette Middle School - The Hill Toppers." Applause rang out as the Hill Toppers stood and waved from their table.

"In second place..." the teacher paused. She stepped away from the microphone for a moment as she compared notes with the other teachers.

"Actually, we have a tie for first place! From Greenfield Middle School, we have the eighth grade Green Fielders and...from Silverbrook Intermediate School - we have the Sea Bees, from, and this is correct, *fifth grade!*"

After a moment to digest this amazing fact, the entire cafeteria erupted with cheers. Lay, Jimmy and Jake stood and waved from their table.

"We decided it would be fun to do this again - you know, to be in another round," Jimmy said, matter-of-factly to an amazed Mrs. Jackson, as the cheers trailed off to a murmur. "So, we signed up for the open-class section."

Mrs. Jackson just smiled and shook her head. "I can't wait to tell Opa," Jake said to his team, as they left the building for the short walk home.

Mark Fralick

28

JOURNEY OR DESTINATION?

The teams getting ready for the citywide *Power Round* had mostly fitful nights of sleep that night. The Saturday competition meant a trip to the State Tournament.

Excited to share the story with his uncle Owen, now serving with the Marines in a far away land, Lay stayed up late to write a letter. He wrote about how the day's competition played out.

As Lay, Jimmy, and Jake walked into the sections, they paused. They'd planned to take on the sixth graders, but just as they were about to turn down that hallway, Jimmy said, "You know, the only way we get to do this more than once, is if we try for the Power Round on Saturday."

After glancing down the hallway, he continued. "There's no rule that tells us how to choose; but I know a journey is something we cannot lose."

Opa talked a lot about the idea of being a *journey person* or a *destination person*.

"Destination people are really quite easy to see,"

Opa once rhymed. "They collect trophies and ribbons; building a monument to *me*. But a journey person's walls are filled with different glories; pictures of challenges, friends and images telling stories. We are all blessed with the gift of having a soul; just what we learn from this journey - that is the goal."

The boys looked at each other. They knew, full well, that heading to the open-class section meant going up against much older middle-school kids.

Without another word, the *Sea Bees* team turned and made their way to the open-class section, and to the puzzled stares of the older kids in that classroom.

"Yeah, we know..." Lay said, dryly, to the curious and questioning eyes.

With that, they sat down and took on the seventh and eighth graders. There were some very hard questions on the test, but only one or two that they didn't know how to attack.

It had been a great day for Lay and his teammates. He paused a moment to burn the memories into his mind as he closed out the letter with his usual request to his uncle; for him to stay safe and return home soon.

Hardly able to keep his eyes open any longer, Lay hopped into bed and fell, swiftly, to sleep.

29

SATURDAY MOURNING

Saturday morning, teams entering the Power Round met in the cafeteria at Silverbrook. Excitement filled the air as students from all over the city packed into the large, echoing room.

Huddled around the many tables, teams and their teachers discussed strategies and worked on practice tests. Lay and Jimmy busily worked sample problems as Mrs. Jackson met them at the table.

"Boys?" she began. The boys saw that Mrs. Jackson looked very serious, and that Madison trailed her by a few steps.

"I got a call from Jake's mom. I am afraid I have some bad news. Jake won't be able to make it this morning. His grandfather is not doing very well. I thought that you two could still continue in the Power Round with Madison filling in for Jake."

The boys had other plans. As soon as they heard about Jake's grandfather they, without a word, began packing themselves up and putting on their jackets.

"We won't be doing that," Jimmy said seriously.

Mrs. Jackson, now trying to make the best of a difficult situation, implored them. "Really boys, I wish you would stay. I think this is a great opportunity for the two of you."

"Opportunity?" Lay asked, as he tossed his backpack over his shoulder, not offering her the option to talk them out of leaving.

"It is the opportunity we will pursue, but probably different than the one thought by you. We have a simple rule that we cannot bend; never miss an opportunity to be there for your friend."

As the boys exited the cafeteria, Madison shot Mrs. Jackson a look as if to say *I told you so.* The boys quickly left the building and jogged the short distance to Jake's house.

Jimmy and Lay went directly to the back door of Jake's house, their usual entrance. Jake's mom, making breakfast for Emily, saw the two boys through the window and motioned them in.

She smiled softly at them but her eyes were red and sad.

"Upstairs," she said, pressing back tears. "Jake is with him..."

They opened the door to Jake's room and found Jake lying next to Opa in his bed, holding his hand and talking about yesterday's events.

"And, we were right," Jake said to Opa, "there were two questions on standard deviation." Jake waved the boys into the room.

"And how did you do on them?" Opa asked softly.

"Nailed them, of course!" Jimmy blurted loudly.

The boys all laughed as Opa smiled broadly,

squinting his eyes the way he always did when he was happy. The boys fell silent for a moment. Opa could see each of them taking a memory snapshot of this moment.

In this very same moment, he was certain of the fact that it was the boys who were now the teachers. They had kept him from despair and taught him that optimism is not just for the young. He was happy, as his lads did not despair still.

"I would like to hear that story now," Opa said softly, closing his eyes, still smiling.

Jake, gently holding his grandfather's hand, began.
There once was a wave, upon the sea so blue,
up and around he moved and others moved too;
for a long time they swam, laughed and did play,
all the time thinking, together they'd stay;
But one day they saw a scary image ahead,
to the shore and jagged rocks they'd be led;

With that, Lay took over:
Don't worry, came a voice, soft yet strong,
if you think this is the end, then you'd be very wrong;
It's easy to think that we're just waves and nothing more,
that our life together is lost and not as before;
But there is a truth that you all may have missed,
though it is often ignored and is easily dismissed;

With a pause, Jimmy started:
In our lives, we move along, and passing go the days,
rolling and rolling through life like in some kind of maze;
This is a story that's been passed since days of old,
seeing an end in our future and feeling fear untold;
But the thing that lies ahead of you is not truly the end,
but just a change we must abide and only one's self send;

Jimmy looked back at Jake now, who would finish the story:

No, my child, said the voice - there's no need to fear,
though this time of change draws ever more near,
You see yourself as a wave because it's an easy thing to believe,
as the bigger thing you're part of - is difficult to conceive;

No, we are not just waves, tossed by the wind and calmed by
the lee...

Something far, far greater, we are the life, the deep...
we are the ever endless sea.

He ended with four quiet words. "We love you, Opa."

30

THE WAY FORWARD

As the days grew longer and the school year came to a close, not a day went by that Jake did not think of his grandfather. Opa used to speak of how when you lose someone you love, it's like they become part of you.

In quiet moments, you can feel closer to them than ever seemed possible before. This is how it was for Jake. He smiled to himself, thinking about Opa.

Glancing out the window of his bedroom on this sunny morning, he saw his friends coming up the sidewalk.

"Got to go, Opa!" he said to the picture carefully situated on his desk. Jake flew from the room, leaving the portrait of a handsome man, with clever eyes, clad in perfect Navy *Dress Whites*, held in the silence of his room.

"Hey, guys!" Jake said, running up to the group. "Hey, Jake!" came the response from Lay, Jimmy and Howie. Yes, Howie, no longer hanging out with Frankie, had become great friends with the boys and was now part of their group. Lay and Howie tossed a football on their way to school, shoving each other off the sidewalk. Jake and Jimmy, with Emily on his shoulders, squawked loudly at each other.

"I think Einstein was smart as a *FOX*," Jake shot at Jimmy.

Jimmy paused as they passed a crossing guard and said, "Because the way he thought of his formula was with a photon in a *BOX*."

"Oh, that was too easy!" yelled Lay from ahead of them. He tossed the football back to Howie. "How about this one? To calculate a circle's circumference there can be *NO DEBATE*..." Lay said loudly, glancing back at Jake and Jimmy.

Jimmy jumped on this one. "Talk about easy, you need to use," he said. "3.1415926535....*EIGHT*!" Jake and Jimmy said in unison.

All the boys laughed, not really caring if the crossing guard, or anyone else, was listening. "Three, fighhhh, eight!" agreed a giggling Emily, with one hand on Jimmy's head and the other raising a fist in the air as she shouted the last digit.

"I have one," said Howie, passing the football to Lay. "Guess who is listening; everyone! Even the *BIRDS*," Howie started hesitantly. "And I can't believe I am hanging out with such giant *NERDS*!"

A boisterous groan erupted from the group along with a single word. "Burn!" Lay snorted, as this laughing group of boys and one smiling little girl made their way forward.

Mark Fralick

ABOUT THE AUTHOR

Mark Fralick, grandson of one of the original officers of
the US Navy Sea Bees, grew up in the Milwaukee and West
Bend areas of Wisconsin. Now living in Texas with his
family, Fralick is a husband, father, software designer,
business owner and proud alumnus of the Madison Scouts
and University of Wisconsin - Green Bay.

www.ingramcontent.com/pod-product-compliance
Lightning Source LLC
Chambersburg PA
CBHW060506030426
42337CB00015B/1760